Brighten up an otherwise bleak mail day with these softly colored postcards.

patterns on pages 26-28

Crazy Quilts
with Hearts and Lace

SEE YOU AT THE QUILTING BEE!

STILL CRAZY AFTER ALL THESE QUILTS

LIFE, LIBERTY, AND THE PURSUIT OF FABRIC

A LITTLE BIRDIE TOLD ME...

come sit with me by the garden gate, we'll visit there... my work can wait

A TIME TO MEND

SEW · MEND
MEND · SEW

A TIME TO SEW

On happy days

when I can stitch

my life runs smooth

without a hitch

BIRDS OF A FEATHER STITCH TOGETHER

HERE'S A CARD MADE JUST FOR YOU

A LOVING THANKS FOR ALL YOU DO

What a wonderful way to turn scraps of fabric leftover from your latest project into thoughtful mail for beloved friends.
patterns on pages 28-31
and on pages 31-33

Fabulous Folk Art
with Fabric and Felt

A PIN IN THE CUSHION IS WORTH TWO IN THE CHAIR

WELCOME

A HOME WITHOUT A DOG IS JUST A HOUSE

Blessings to Ewe

If all my wishes could come true You'd find yours would be granted too...For that is what I've wished for you.

It's not easy being QUEEN

A WOMAN'S WORK

IS NEVER DONE

Come check out my stash

Thank You

BEST WISHES

IF I HAD A SINGLE FLOWER FOR EVERY TIME I THINK ABOUT YOU, I COULD WALK FOREVER IN MY GARDEN.

Kind thoughts and varied interests can all be woven into your own special Post Card design.

patterns on pages 33-36

and on pages 36-38

Special Sentiments
for Family and Friends

The one who dies with the most fabric wins

With pins and needles

So much fabric... so little time

Post Card

Dear Diana,
Just a note to
let you know I was
thinking of you.
Sincerely,
Connie

D. Mc ...
P. O. B...
H. ...

Specialty Cards
for Fabric Lovers
and Quilters

Whether your style is soft and subtle or bright and colorful, you'll find a Post Card design that's the perfect fit.

patterns on pages 39-40

and on pages 40-42

Sisters are special

I hope you feel better soon

When life gives you scraps, make a quilt

#1 Teacher

In the crazy quilt of life, I'm glad you're in my block of friends.

Quilting is my passion

Post Card

Dear Suzanne,
Here's wishing you a
Happy Birthday.
Always,
Kirsty

S. McNeill
2425 Cullen St.
Fort Worth, TX
76107

YOU ARE MY SUNSHINE

Quilting with a friend will keep you in stitches

You're my best friend

Friends are the fabric of life

Capture the colors of spring and send them across the miles to someone special.

patterns on pages 43-45

and on pages 46-47

Friendship Cards
for Quilt and Fabric Lovers

How does your garden grow?... with wonderful bunnies and lovely lace trims!

patterns on pages 48-49

and on pages 50-52

Love Letters

from the Heart

Have time to stitch?

BLEST BE THE TIES

Let's trade buttons

Creative minds are rarely tidy.

Thanks for everything

Quilters aren't greedy, They're just materialistic!

Capture the colors of fall and send them across the miles to someone special.

patterns on pages 52-55

and on pages 56-58

Fall Friendships
for All Occasions

Cards of Joy
for the Holiday Season

Stitch the colors of the season into a
warm expression of your friendship.

patterns on pages 59-60

and pages 63-64

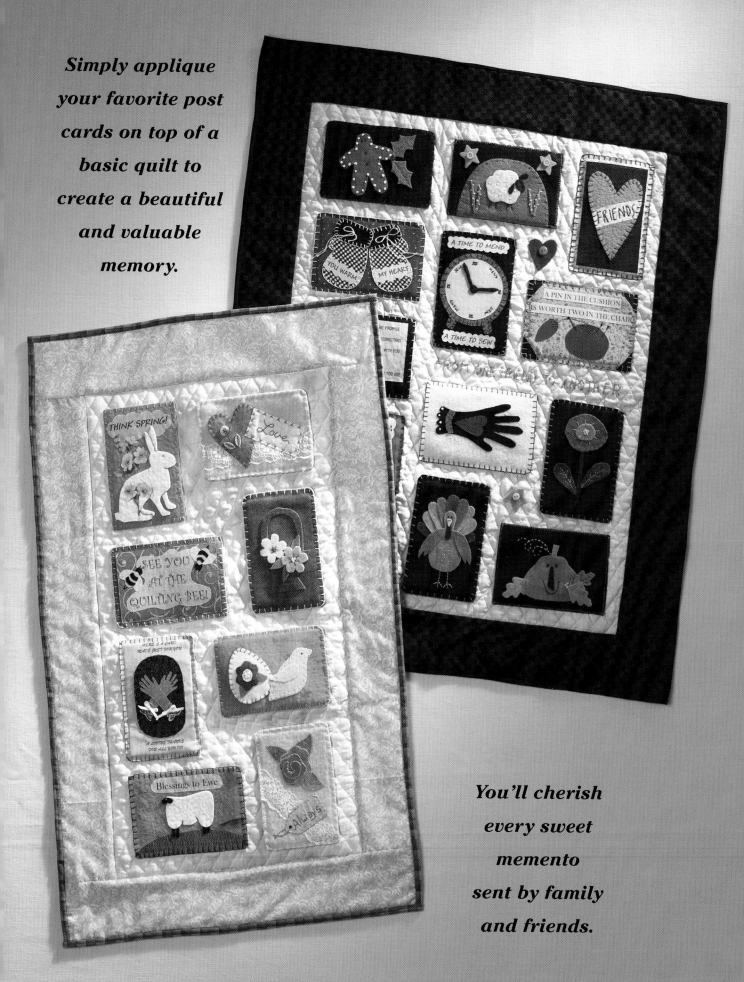

Simply applique your favorite post cards on top of a basic quilt to create a beautiful and valuable memory.

You'll cherish every sweet memento sent by family and friends.

Post Card Quilts

I love every post card that has been sent to me by a friend. After I received a dozen or so, I started thinking about what I could do with them... they are just too wonderful to hide away in a box. So, I made a basic quilt and simply appliqued my favorite cards on top.

Pink Post Cards Quilt

Finished size: 20^1/2" x 31"

Materials:
1 yard Pre-quilted muslin
^{1}/2 yard Pink border
^{1}/6 yard Green binding

Cutting:
Pre-quilted muslin:
  14" x 24^1/2" for top
  21" x 32" for backing
2 Pink side border strips 3^1/2" x 24^1/2"
2 Pink top/bottom border strips 3^1/2" x 20"
Cut 2^1/2" wide Green binding strips and
  sew together for 108"

Construction:
  Choose 4 vertical and 4 horizontal designs. Arrange them on pre-quilted fabric.
  Pin in place. Hand stitch in place.
  Sew the side borders to the quilt.
  Sew top and bottom borders to the quilt.
  Pin the top and backing together.
  Quilt as desired.
  Fold the binding in half, lengthwise, wrong sides together. Press.
  Sew to the front of the quilt, with raw edges together.
  Turn to the back. Sew in place.

Black Post Cards Quilt

Finished size: 26^1/2" x 31^1/2"

Materials:
1^1/3 yard Pre-quilted muslin
^{1}/2 yard Black print border
^{1}/6 yard Black solid binding
2" square felt (Red, Gold) for heart and star
Buttons (^{1}/2" Red, ^{3}/8" Gold)
Green pearl cotton

Cutting:
Pre-quilted muslin:
  20" x 25" for top
  27" x 32" for backing
2 Black side border strips 3^1/2" x 25"
2 Black top/bottom border strips 3^1/2" x 26^1/2"
Cut 2^1/2" wide Black binding strips and sew
  together for 118"

Construction:
  Choose 4 vertical and 9 horizontal designs. Arrange them on pre-quilted fabric.
  Pin in place. Hand stitch in place.
  Cut a star from gold wool. Hand stitch in place, adding a gold button.
  Cut a heart from red felt. Hand stitch in place, adding a red button.
  Backstitch "From One Friend to Another" with green pearl cotton.
  Sew the side borders to the quilt.
  Sew top and bottom borders to the quilt.
  Pin the top and backing together.
  Quilt as desired.
  Fold the binding in half, lengthwise, wrong sides together. Press.
  Sew to the front of the quilt, with raw edges together.
  Turn to the back. Sew in place.

General Instructions

These post cards are a wonderful way to send a special, personalized message to a friend or relative.

Because they are standard post card size (4" x 6"), they could also be easily placed in a decorative frame to preserve them forever.

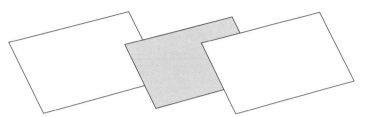

Cut a 4" x 6" rectangle from background fabric.

Cut a $3^{1}/2$" x $5^{1}/2$" rectangle on Steam-A-Seam 2.

Place a decorated post card front on top. Press with iron.

The post cards are basically made by placing two 4" x 6" pieces of fabric together with a $3^{1}/2$" x $5^{1}/2$" piece of stabilizer (stiffener) sandwiched in between. For stabilizer, we suggest using poster board, shirt weight cardboard, a $3^{1}/2$" x $5^{1}/2$" index card, or 70 weight Pellon.

Fuse the layers together: apply Steam A Seam II (fusible web) to the back sides of the two 4" x 6" fabric pieces, place the $3^{1}/2$" x $5^{1}/2$" stabilizer in the middle of the two pieces, and iron together.

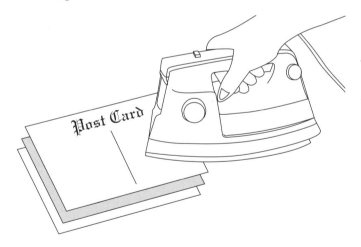

Assembling the Post Cards

NOTE:
Be sure to remove the paper backings from all of the fusible web.

Layer the pieces of your post card as follows: Front, right side down. Center the $3^{1}/2$" x $5^{1}/2$" stabilizer piece (poster board, index card, 70 weight Pellon, or shirt weight cardboard) on top of the front piece. Place the back piece (wrong side down) on top of the stabilizer. Using the Craft and Appliqué sheet (optional), iron the card so all layers are fused together.

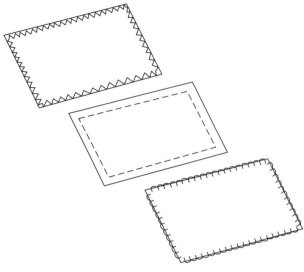

Finishing

To finish the edges of a post card:
Use the zig-zag stitch on your sewing machine;
Use a Running Stitch with Pearl Cotton; or
Do a Blanket stitch (Buttonhole stitch) all around the edges using Pearl Cotton, thread, or embroidery floss.

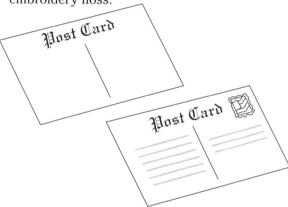

Prepare the Back

Use a pre-printed Post Card muslin backing from Design Originals or print your own back.
Note: To print your own messages, use fabric sheets for inkjet printers OR iron freezer paper onto one side of muslin. Then use your computer to print "Post Card" or a message on the back before assembling the card.
Use a Micron #05 Black permanent pen to write a message.

Invitations and Notes: Print information on the back of several cards before assembling.

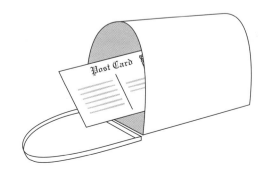

Post Card

Place a Postage Stamp here

Pre-printed muslin fabric with 'Post Card' printed on it for the backing is available from Design Originals.

General Materials Needed for Basic Post Cards:

Scraps of cotton fabrics, wool, or felt

Stabilizer, which could be an index card, shirt weight cardboard, poster board, or 70 weight Pellon.

Steam A Seam II fusible web

**Craft and Appliqué Sheet ™ (optional but very helpful)

Light table (optional but very helpful)

Iron and ironing board

Micron Pigma Pens-size 02 or 03 in black or other colors

Additional Materials (optional):

Colored pencils, crayons, acrylic paint

Mod Podge

Small paintbrush

Hot glue gun and sticks, suitable for fabric

Pearl cotton, embroidery floss

Matching threads

Plastic template

Fabric sheets for inkjet printers

Embellishments:
Such as buttons, beads, ribbon, lace, decorative thread, diamond dust or glitter.

Post Card

**The Craft and Appliqué Sheet™

The Craft and Appliqué Sheet™ is a 13" x 17" transparent, non-stick reusable sheet for all craft and pressing applications. It is very helpful for quick fuse appliqué and also has many other uses. It can be used under a hot glue gun to catch drips which will easily peel off and also releases paint and modeling clay. It is dishwasher and oven safe. Food will not stick to it. The Craft and Appliqué Sheet™ wipes off easily and rolls up for handy storage.

**The Craft and Appliqué Sheet™ is available from www.prairiegrovepeddler.com

Pen Stitch
Post Cards

These post cards have the sayings "stitched" with a pen.

Trace the templates onto clear plastic. Cut out the shapes. Use these templates to cut out the shapes after you trace the words onto the fabric

You will need to use a light color cotton fabric on which to trace the words.
Press Steam A Seam 2 (fusible web) to the back of your fabric.
Using a light table, trace the words onto the fabric using a Micron Pigma Pen-size 02 or 03 in black or your choice of color.

Center the plastic template over the traced words and trace around the shape. Cut out inside the traced line.

Pen stitch lines $1/8$" inside the outer edge. Peel paper backing off and press to post card.

General Directions -
Pen Stitch and Color Post Cards

Just as the name says, these post cards are "stitched" with a pen and then colored in.

For each post card you will need:
2 pieces of muslin: 4" x 6" (front and back of post card)

1 piece of poster board or shirt weight cardboard: $3^1/2$" x $5^1/2$" (this will be placed in-between the front and back of the card to stabilize it)

Steam-A-Seam 2: Cut two 4" x 6" (these will be placed on the muslin pieces as the card is assembled)

Micron Pigma Pen - Size 02 - Black

Crayons, colored pencils or acrylic paint. (white crayons and colored pencils should not be used)

Diamond Dust or glass glitter

Mod Podge

Small paintbrush

Place one piece of muslin on top of the template.
Trace the design onto your muslin using the #02 pigma pen.

Colored Designs for Post Cards

For colors: Color the design using crayons, colored pencils or acrylic paint.

For paint: Dry brush the areas you wish to paint, rather than painting them a solid color. Simply dip your brush in the paint, wipe most of it off on a paper towel, then paint.

Crayons and colored pencils:
It's as simple as using a coloring book! White color pencils and crayons do not show up well on fabric, so we suggest using acrylic paint for all white areas of a design.

After the design has been colored in, you may wish to go over some of the smaller detail lines again with your Pigma pen.

Using a paintbrush, lightly place Mod Podge anywhere you'd like to have some glitter. Sprinkle on the glitter generously and let dry. Wipe off the excess.

Assembly

Place fusible web on the back sides of both pieces of muslin.

Layer the card as follows:
Front of the card, fusible web side up, place the cardboard on top of that and then place the back of the card, fusible web side down. Square off all edges if needed. Iron the front and back of the card so all three pieces adhere to one another.

Sew around the edges of the card using a zig-zag stitch on your sewing machine.

Post Cards with Inkjet Printed Sayings

General Directions:
These post cards are made with sayings that are printed directly on fabric using an inkjet printer. You will need to purchase "fabric sheets for inkjet printers" which are available at many craft stores or printing/copy centers.

The instructions given for each post card will indicate the font type and size used in the picture shown. You will need to format the saying as shown in the picture so it will fit in the surrounding shape.

Follow the manufacturer's directions for printing on the fabric sheets.

Unless otherwise instructed, once the saying is printed on the fabric, you will be applying Steam-A-Seam 2 (fusible web) to the back side of the printed fabric saying and cutting out a shape. It is very helpful to use a light box (or a window) so you can see the printed words when applying the Steam-A-Seam 2 to the back of the printed fabric piece.

Alternative:
If you do not wish to print the words using a computer, you could trace the words onto a piece of muslin using a Micron Pigma Pen-size 02 or 03 in black.

Quilted Fabric
Post Cards

Quilt post cards are made by backing pieces of fabric to fusible web and then fitting the pieces together, much like a puzzle. Additional appliqué pieces can then be fused on top of the foundation piece, along with buttons, lace, etc. The front is then joined to the back with a piece of shirt weight cardboard or poster board between the layers to stabilize the post card.

When using the templates provided, please note that the dashed line approximately $1/4$" from the edge represents the finished size of 4" x 6."

See directions for using fusible web before beginning your crazy quilt post cards. It is important to remember that when transferring the various pieces onto the fusible web, you must reverse them. To do this, place the fusible web over the template and trace the shapes. Flip the web over, and retrace over those lines. Add the numbers as shown on the template.

Remove the paper backing from the side that does not have the numbers, and stick that side to your fabric pieces.

For each post card you will need:
2 pieces of muslin: 5" x 7" (front and back of post card)

1 piece of poster board or unlined index card or piece of 70 weight Pellon or shirt weight cardboard cut to $3^1/2$" x $5^1/2$" (this will be placed between the front and back of the card to stabilize it)

Steam-A-Seam 2: Cut two 5" x 7" (these will be placed on the muslin pieces as the card is assembled)

You will also need, small pieces of fabric, one for each number on the template and appliqué pieces as well as additional Steam-A-Seam 2.

Once you have traced the pieces onto your fusible web and placed them on your fabric, cut out the fabric pieces. Following the template, remove the paper backing from the fusible web & place the fabric onto one piece of your 5" x 7" muslin.

To embellish the card, use your sewing machine, or 2 strands of floss and embroidery stitches and stitch between each different piece of fabric, much like you see on a crazy quilt. Add any additional appliqué pieces once they have been backed with fusible web. Iron the front of the card using a pressing sheet.

Sew on buttons, lace, etc., where required. If there is hand stitching for lettering, do that now using 2 strands of floss.

When the front of the card is completed, place the 5" x 7" piece of fusible web on the back. Place the other 5" x 7" piece of fusible web on the other piece of 5" x 7" muslin.
Lay these two pieces on top of one another and cut off approximately $1/2$" from either side so both pieces now measure 4" x 6."

Assemble post card following general instructions on page 20.

Let's share
fat quarters

Wanna stitch?

The one who dies
with the most fabric
wins

You've got me
busting at the seams

Thank You
for the gift

I missed
you at the
Guild Meeting

Hope you
feel better

Wool
Post Cards

Each wool post card contains a front/foundation, middle and back piece. Felt may be substituted for hand-dyed wool.

For all post cards regardless of the design, you will need:

2 pieces of wool : 4" x 6" (front & back of card)

1 piece of muslin: 3 1/2" x 5 1/2" (back of post card - this area is where the address will be written)

(Alternative: use one piece of 4" x 6" wool for front of card and one piece of 4" x 6" muslin for back of card)

1 piece of 3 1/2" x 5 1/2" liner (poster board, unlined index card, 70 weight Pellon, or shirt weight cardboard). This will be placed between the front and back of the card to stabilize it.

You will also need Steam A Seam 2 fusible web cut into the following sizes:

Cut two 3 1/2" x 5 1/2"

Cut one 3 1/2" x 5 1/2" (Note: you will not need this if you are using a 4" x 6" muslin piece for the post card back)

Assorted pieces of wool for appliqué, buttons, floss & Pearl Cotton thread (see the individual pattern directions).

All appliqué pieces should be backed with fusible web. It is important to remember that when transferring the various shapes onto the fusible web, you must reverse them. To do this, place the fusible web over the template and trace the shapes. Flip the web over, and retrace over those lines. Place an X on this side of the web. When you place the fusible web on your fabric, place the side that does not have the X. Cut out your appliqué pieces and place them on the front of the card. See individual directions and pictures for correct placement, stitching instructions, floss used, etc.

Return to this page when you have completed the front of your wool card.

Assembling a Post Card

(Note: You may skip this first step if you are using a 4" x 6" muslin piece for the back of the post card).

Place the 3 1/2" x 5 1/2" piece of fusible web on one side of the 3 1/2" x 5 1/2" piece of muslin. With the muslin facing up, center this piece on top of the back piece of your post card. Following the manufacturer's instructions for the fusible web, iron these two pieces together.

Do a decorative or zig-zag stitch around the edges.

Place the two 3 1/2" x 5 1/2" pieces of fusible web on either side of the 3 1/2" x 5 1/2" piece of stabilizer (cardboard or Pellon).

Place the front of the post card face down.

Remove the paper backing from the fusible web you've placed on the cardboard and center it on the wrong side of the post card front. With the muslin side facing up, place the back of the post card on top of the cardboard, making sure it's centered.

Iron the post card, using a pressing cloth.

Finish the Card

To finish around the edges of the post card, do either a blanket stitch using #5 Pearl Cotton, or do a zig-zag stitch using your sewing machine.

Enjoy life!

Quilters know
how to enjoy life

My life is in pieces

Pin pals

Glad you're back!

That vacation
was so long

Wish you were here!

From one grandma
to another!

Stitchin' Chicks

See page 22 for PEN STITCH basic supplies & assembly.
ADDITIONAL SUPPLIES: 4" x 6" of red and white polka dot fabric • Scraps of gold cotton and black print
INSTRUCTIONS: Words are printed with Baskerville Old Face, size 36 bold. • Trace one egg and two chicks IN REVERSE on Steam-A-Seam 2. Roughly cut out around lines and remove backing. Finger press pieces onto back side of fabrics. Cut on traced lines and remove paper backing. • Position words, chicks, and egg on background fabric. Iron in place. • With black floss or thread, make stitch marks around chicks and eggs, backstitch chick legs, and make French knots for eyes. • Following general directions, continue with post card assembly. • Buttonhole stitch around post card with black floss or thread.

Don't Count Your Chickens

See page 22 for PEN STITCH basic supplies & assembly.
ADDITIONAL SUPPLIES: 4" x 6" of background fabric (red) • Scraps of two shades of pink, black, yellow
INSTRUCTIONS: Words are printed in Kristen ITC, size 22 bold italic. • Position words on lower edge of post card. Iron in place. • Trace chicken, tail, comb, beak, wattle, and three eggs IN REVERSE onto Steam-A-Seam 2. Roughly cut around traced line and remove backing. Finger press pieces to back side of fabrics and cut out on lines. Remove paper backings. • Position beak, comb, wattle, tail, and body on background. Iron in place. • Position eggs and iron in place. • Cut a 3 1/2" x 5 1/2" piece of Pellon and glue to back of background. • Using two strands of floss, make a single French knot for eye and double French knots on tail where indicated by dots. • Following general directions, continue the post card assembly. • Buttonhole stitch around post card edge with one strand of floss.

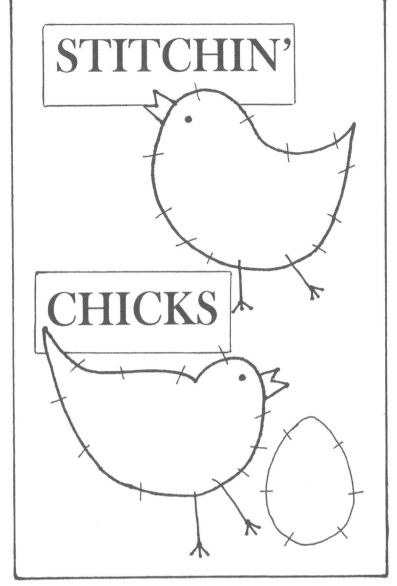

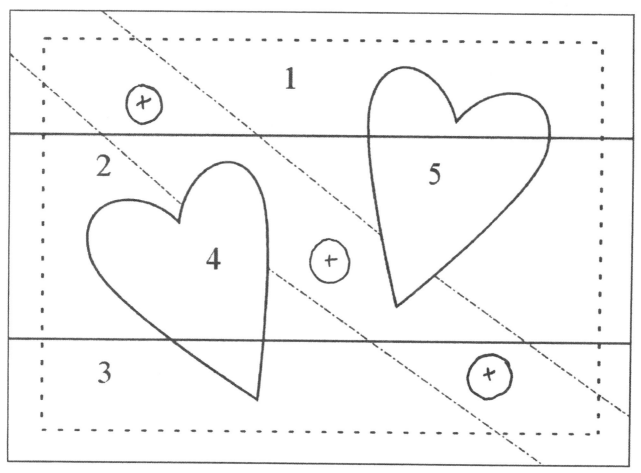

Hearts and Lace

See page 23 for QUILT basic supplies & assembly.

ADDITIONAL SUPPLIES: 3 fabric scraps for background • Floral fabric for 2 hearts • 8" of $1^{1/4}$" lace • Three $5/8$" buttons • Cream thread

INSTRUCTIONS: Cut a 5" x 7" piece of muslin. Cut strips from Steam-A-Seam 2, press to backs of background strips and cut out.

Press to background. Zig-zag along edges of strips. • Place lace diagonally across post card and tack in place. • Cut hearts from Steam-A-Seam 2. Remove backings and press to back side of floral fabric. Cut out on lines. Position on card and press. Zig-zag around edges of hearts. • Sew buttons in place on lace. • Follow general directions to complete post card.

Always

See page 24 for WOOL basic supplies & assembly.

ADDITIONAL SUPPLIES: Wool fabric (Off-White, 3 shades Mauve, Green).
• 2" x 3" prairie cloth
• Embroidery floss (Green, Pink, Brown, Tan)
• Ecru Pearl Cotton
• $1^{1/4}$" x 6" flat lace.

INSTRUCTIONS: Sew lace onto card. Trim excess.
• Position leaves and rose pieces. Using 2-ply floss: Appliqué rose using pink and blanket stitch. Appliqué leaves using green and straight stitch.
• Trace "Always" onto prairie cloth. Stitch using 2-ply green.
• Cut around outline of tag. Blanket stitch to card using 2-ply tan. • Draw circle on tag using Black Pigma pen. Stitch string using 2-ply brown.
• Blanket stitch edging using ecru Pearl Cotton.
• Follow general directions to complete post card.

Mothers Are Like Roses ▲

See page 22 for PEN STITCH basic supplies & assembly.
ADDITIONAL SUPPLIES: 4" x 6" of burgundy • 2$^{1}/2$" piece of 1$^{3}/8$" wide lace • Thread to match lace • Gold embroidery floss • 3$^{1}/2$" fabric square with rose motif
INSTRUCTIONS: Print words on fabric. Pattern was printed in Fine Hand, size 24 bold. • Trace four rectangles on Steam-A-Seam 2. Roughly cut around lines and remove backing. Finger press to back. Cut on lines and remove paper backing. Position on background fabric, but do not iron. • Trace rectangle for floral motif on Steam-A-Seam 2. Roughly cut around lines and remove backing. Finger press rectangle to back of rose motif. Cut out on lines and remove paper backing. Position on background, but do not iron. • Position lace at an angle on background fabric, mitering bottom edge under words. • Iron pieces on background. From back side, make a few stitches to secure lace edges to background. • With one strand of floss, buttonhole stitch around the rose motif. • Follow general directions to complete post card. • Buttonhole stitch around post card using one strand of floss.

Heart In Hand ▶

See page 24 for WOOL basic supplies & assembly.
ADDITIONAL SUPPLIES: Wool fabric (4" x 6" of Off-White, scraps of Black, Red, Grey) • Embroidery floss (Off-White, Black)
INSTRUCTIONS: Trace hand, heart, and cuff IN REVERSE on Steam-A-Seam 2. Roughly cut around lines and remove backing. Finger press pieces to back of fabrics. Cut on lines and remove paper backing. • Position hand, heart and cuff on background and iron. • Make a French knot on each scallop with Off-White embroidery floss. • Follow general directions to complete post card. • Buttonhole stitch around edge with black floss.

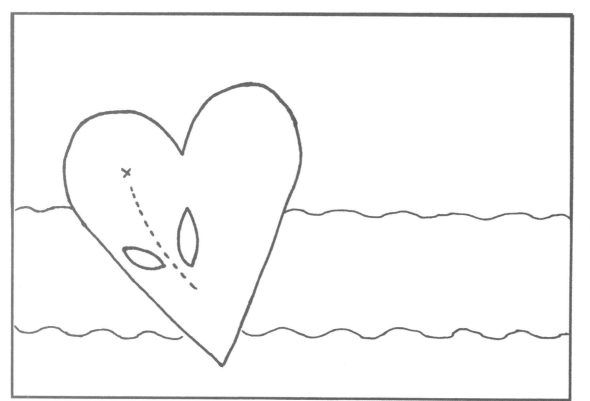

Love

See page 24 for WOOL basic supplies & assembly.
ADDITIONAL SUPPLIES: Wool fabric (Off white, Rose, Green) • $1^1/2$" x 3" muslin for embroidery. • Green embroidery floss • Ecru pearl cotton • $1^1/2$" x 6" lace • $1^1/2$" button

INSTRUCTIONS: Sew lace onto card. • Using 2-ply floss, appliqué heart with blanket stitch. Attach leaves with straight stitch. • Draw stem with chalk and stitch. • Sew bottom to top of stem. Trace "Love" onto muslin and stitch. • Place rectangle onto post card and stitch around edges. • Edge with blanket stitch, using ecru Pearl Cotton. • Follow general directions to complete post card.

See You At the Quilting Bee

See pages 23 for QUILT basic supplies & assembly.
ADDITIONAL SUPPLIES: 4" x 6" each of purple for background and green print for inner background • Scraps of yellow, black, gold fabrics • Black embroidery floss • Yellow Pearl Cotton
INSTRUCTIONS: Print words on fabric sheet. Pattern was printed in Curlz MT, size 48 bold. • Trace words piece on Steam-A-Seam 2. Roughly cut around lines and remove backing. Finger press to back side on printed fabric. Cut out on line and remove paper backing. Position words on post card and iron. • Trace 2 bee bodies, 2 sets of wings, 2 heads, and 4 stripes (2 of each size) on Steam-A-Seam 2. Roughly cut around lines and remove backing. Finger press pieces to back of fabrics. Cut out and remove the paper backing. • Position bee wings, then heads, then bodies, then stripes on post card and iron. • Using 2-ply embroidery floss, make small stitches at top of each head and tail for "feelers" and "stingers". • Follow general directions to complete post card. • Buttonhole stitch around post card edge using yellow Pearl cotton.

Crazy Quilt

See page 23 for QUILT basic supplies & assembly.

ADDITIONAL SUPPLIES: 4" x 6" of crazy quilt fabric or muslin and various scraps to make background • Embroidery floss
INSTRUCTIONS: Print words onto fabric. Pattern is printed in Andy , size 22 bold italic. • Trace words pattern IN REVERSE onto Steam-A-Seam 2 and roughly cut around piece. Remove backing and finger press on back of fabric. Cut on line and remove paper backing. • Position words onto background and iron. With floss, buttonhole stitch around the word piece. • Follow general directions to complete post card. • Buttonhole stitch around outer edge with floss.

LIFE, LIBERTY,

AND THE PURSUIT OF FABRIC

Life & Liberty Flag

See page 23 for QUILT basic supplies & assembly.

ADDITIONAL SUPPLIES: 4" x 6" of Red print with stars • Scrap of navy print with stars • Gold embroidery floss
INSTRUCTIONS: Print words on fabric. Pattern was printed in Colonna MT, size 28 bold. • Trace words pieces (stripes) onto Steam-A-Seam 2. Roughly cut around lines. Finger press pieces to back of words. Cut on lines and remove paper backing. Position word pieces on background. • Trace star piece on Steam-A-Seam 2. Roughly cut around lines. Finger press to back of the navy fabric. Cut on line and remove paper backing. Position on background. • Iron pieces to background. • Follow general directions to complete post card. • Buttonhole stitch around edge with one strand of gold embroidery floss.

Blue Flower

See page 24 WOOL basic supplies & assembly.
ADDITIONAL SUPPLIES: Wool fabric (Black, Blue, Gold, Dark Green, Medium Green) • Embroidery floss (Gold, Green, Blue)
INSTRUCTIONS: Appliqué top of card: Back stem and leaves with fusible web. Place the stem and 2 leaves on background and iron. • With 2-ply floss, stitch veins in leaves • Blanket stitch center of flower onto blue wool. Blanket stitch flower onto front of card, overlapping stem slightly. • Make straight stitches from under center of flower in gold. • Using 6-ply floss make 5 French knots in center of flower. • Follow general directions to complete post card. • Edge card with blanket stitch using 6-ply blue floss.

A Little Birdie Told Me

See page 22 for PEN STITCH basic supplies & assembly.
ADDITIONAL SUPPLIES: 5" x 6" of blue cotton • Scraps of yellow and black fabric • Pigma pen • Yellow embroidery floss
INSTRUCTIONS: Print words on fabric sheet. Pattern shown was printed in Californian FB, size 36 bold italic. • Trace 3" x 5" rectangle on Steam-A-Seam 2. Roughly cut around lines and remove backing. Finger press rectangle onto back of words. Cut out on traced line. • With Black Pigma pen, trace branches onto printed rectangle. Make dots where indicated. • Remove paper backing from rectangle. Position on background and iron. • IN REVERSE, trace bird body, wing, and beak on Steam-A-Seam 2. Cut out roughly on lines and remove backing. Finger press to back of fabrics. Cut on lines and remove paper backing. Position bird beak, then body, then wing and iron. • Using yellow embroidery floss, make a French knot for eye. • Follow general directions to complete post card. • Buttonhole stitch around post card using yellow embroidery floss.

Come Sit With Me

See page 23 for QUILT basic supplies & assembly.

ADDITIONAL SUPPLIES: Wool or cotton fabric (4" x 6" of Purple; scraps of Gold, Green Red) • Embroidery floss (Green, Black)
INSTRUCTIONS: Print words on fabric sheet. Pattern shown was printed in Vladimir Script, size 26 italic. • Trace garden gate on Steam-A-Seam 2. Roughly cut around line and remove backing. Finger press to back of printed fabric. Cut on line and remove backing. Position on background and iron. With 2-ply green floss, buttonhole stitch around gate. • Trace leaves, tulips, and watering can IN REVERSE on Steam-A-Seam 2. Roughly cut around lines and remove backing. Finger press fabrics and cut on lines. Remove backing. Position on background and iron. • With 2-ply green floss, stitch grass and stems. With 1-ply black floss, backstitch rim of watering can. • Follow general directions to complete post card. • With 2-ply green floss, buttonhole stitch around edge.

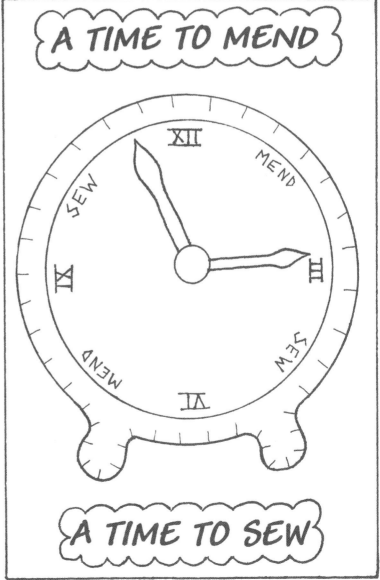

A Time to Mend

See page 23 for QUILT basic supplies & assembly.
ADDITIONAL SUPPLIES: 4" x 6" of wool or cotton fabric (Black, Brown print) • Brown pearl cotton • Black embroidery floss • Quilt marking pencil
INSTRUCTIONS: Print words on fabric. Pattern was printed in Andy, size 28 bold italic. • Trace both scalloped pieces on Steam-A-Seam2. Roughly cut around lines and remove backing. Finger press to back of words. Cut on lines and remove backing. Position on post card. • Trace clock and clock face on Steam-A-Seam 2. Roughly cut around lines and remove backing. Finger press to back of fabrics. Cut on lines and remove backing. Position on card and iron • Trace clock hands and center on Steam-A-Seam 2. Roughly cut around lines and remove backing. Finger press to back of black fabric. Cut on lines and remove backing. Position on clock and iron. • With 1-ply floss, buttonhole stitch around outer edge of clock. • With quilt marking pencil, draw the numerals and words on clock face. Stitch with 1-ply floss. • Follow general directions to complete post card. • Buttonhole stitch around post card with pearl cotton.

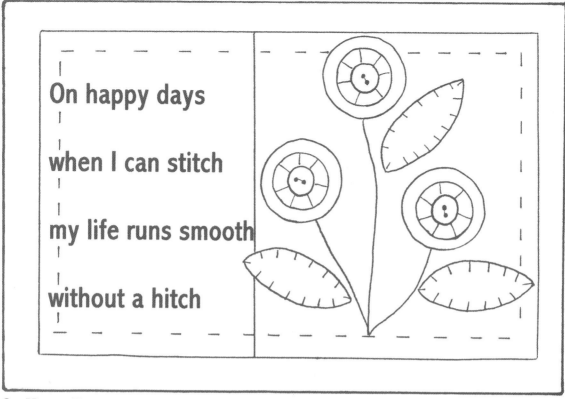

On Happy Days

See page 23 for QUILT basic supplies & assembly.
ADDITIONAL SUPPLIES: 4" x 6" of black wool or cotton • 4" square of floral • Scraps of Black, Brown, Tweed, Tan, Green • Three $3/8$" buttons • Embroidery floss (Black, Gold)
INSTRUCTIONS: Print words on fabric. Pattern was printed in Abadi MT Condensed, size 22 bold. Trace two $3^1/4$" x 3" pieces on Steam-A-Seam 2. Roughly cut around lines and remove backings. Finger press one piece to back of words, and the other to back of floral fabric. Cut on lines and remove backings. • Position on background and iron. • Trace three flower backs, centers, and leaves on Steam-A-Seam-2. Roughly cut around lines and remove backing. Finger press to fabrics. Cut on lines and remove backings. Position pieces on post card and iron. • Using black floss, backstitch flower stems. Buttonhole stitch around flower centers and leaves. Stitch a button in center of each flower. Sew a running stitch around outer edge of inner background. • Follow general directions to complete card. • Buttonhole stitch around edge using gold floss.

Birds of a Feather

See pages 23 for QUILT basic supplies & assembly.
ADDITIONAL SUPPLIES: Cotton fabric (4" x 6" each of brown print & brown solid, Scrap of Black) • Black embroidery floss
INSTRUCTIONS: Cut a 4" x 6" rectangle from brown print. Trace a $3^1/4$" x $5^1/4$" rectangle on Steam-A-Seam 2. Roughly cut around lines and remove backing. Finger press to back of solid brown. Cut on lines and remove backing. Position solid brown over brown print and iron in place. • Print words on fabric. Pattern was printed in Andy, size 28 bold. • Trace words piece on Steam-A-Seam 2. Roughly cut around lines and remove backing. Finger press on back of words. Cut on lines and remove backing. Position on card. • Trace 2 birds on Steam-A-Seam 2. Roughly cut around lines and remove backing. Finger press to back of black fabric. Cut on lines and remove backing. Position on card and iron. • With 2-ply black floss, stitch bird legs and backstitch "string" that birds are holding. Make French knots for eyes. • Follow general directions to complete post card. • Buttonhole stitch around edge with black floss.

Loving Thanks

See page 23 for QUILT basic supplies & assembly.
ADDITIONAL SUPPLIES: Scraps (Black and Gold cotton, nylon lace) • Thread to match lace • 12" of ¹/₈" Ecru ribbon • Black embroidery floss
INSTRUCTIONS: Print words onto fabric, allowing 4¹/₄" between lines of text. Pattern is printed in Brush Script MT, size 18 bold italic. Pencil a 4" x 6" rectangle and cut out. • Trace center oval onto Steam-A-Seam 2, roughly cut and finger press to back of black fabric. Cut out, remove backing, position on background, and iron. • IN REVERSE, trace gloves onto Steam-A-Seam 2, roughly cut and finger press to back of gold fabric. Cut out, remove backing, and position on oval. • Cut two pieces of nylon lace. Position one edge under lower edge of each glove. Iron gloves to oval. From back, make tiny stitches at lace edges to secure. • Using black floss, buttonhole stitch around oval. • Make two bows and stitch one to each glove. • Follow general directions to complete post card. • With 1-ply floss, buttonhole stitch around outer edge.

Welcome Pineapple

See pages 23 for QUILT basic supplies & assembly.
ADDITIONAL SUPPLIES: 4" x 6" of cotton or wool (Black, Gold) • Scrap of Green wool • Pearl cotton (Black, Gold)
INSTRUCTIONS: Cut a 4" x 6" piece from background fabric. • Print word on fabric. Pattern was printed in Monotype Corsiva, size 56 bold italic. • Trace word piece on Steam-A-Seam 2. Roughly cut around lines and remove backing. Finger press to back of word. Cut on lines and remove backing. Position word on post card. • Trace pineapple and leaves IN REVERSE on Steam-A-Seam 2. Roughly cut around lines and remove backing. Finger press to back of fabrics. Cut out on lines and remove backings. Position leaves, then pineapple on background and press. • With black pearl cotton, make lines on pineapple by making single long stitches from left side diagonally across to right side. Make a small stitch (from the back side) at each intersection of the lines to secure.• Follow general directions to complete post card. • Buttonhole stitch around post card using gold pearl.

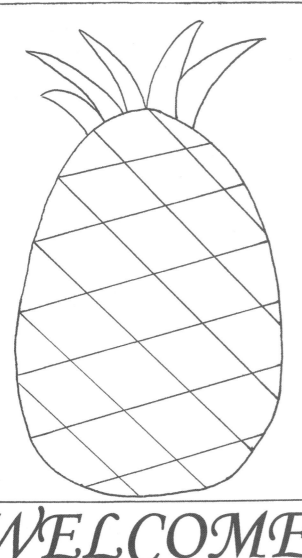

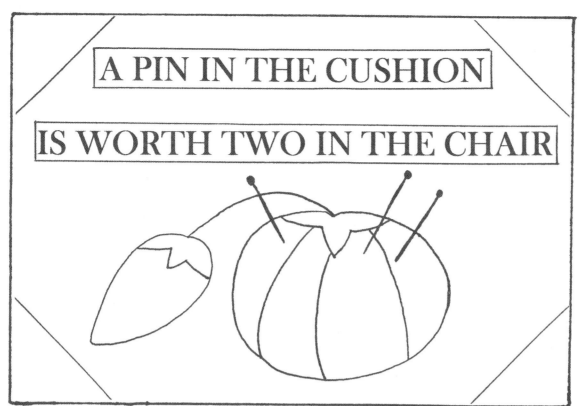

A Pin in the Cushion

See page 23 for QUILT basic supplies & assembly.
ADDITIONAL SUPPLIES: 4" x 6" of Yellow print cotton • Scraps of Red, Green and Black cotton • Embroidery floss (Green, Black) • Quilt marking pencil
INSTRUCTIONS: Cut a 4" x 6" piece from background fabric. • Trace corner pieces on Steam-A-Seam 2. Roughly cut around lines and remove backing. Finger press to back of black. Cut on lines and remove backing. Position and iron. • Print words on fabric. Pattern was printed in Baskerville Old Face, size 26 bold. • Trace word pieces on Steam-A-Seam 2. Roughly cut around pieces and remove backing. Finger press to back of words. Cut on lines and remove backings. Position on background. • IN REVERSE, trace pincushion, pincushion top, strawberry, and strawberry top on Steam-A-Seam 2. Roughly cut around pieces and remove backing. Finger press to fabrics. Cut on lines and remove backings. Iron to background. • Using marking pencil, draw stem and lines on pincushion. Backstitch with 2-ply green floss. With 2-ply black floss, stitch straight lines for pins and make a triple French knot at top of each pin. • Follow general directions to complete post card. • Buttonhole stitch around post card with 2-ply green floss.

Scottie Dogs

See pages 23 for QUILT basic supplies & assembly.
ADDITIONAL SUPPLIES: 4" x 6" of Red wool or cotton • Scraps of Black, Red, and Brown tweed • Embroidery floss (White, Black)
INSTRUCTIONS: Cut a 4" x 6" piece from background fabric. • Print words on fabric. Pattern is printed in Showcard Gothic, size 28 bold. • Trace dog bones onto Steam-A-Seam 2. Roughly cut around lines and remove backing. Finger press to back of words. Cut on lines and remove backing. Position bones on post card. • Trace dogs, collars, and coats onto Steam-A-Seam 2. Roughly cut around lines and remove backing. Finger press to back of fabrics. Cut on lines and remove backing. Position pieces on post card. and iron. • Using white floss, make French knots for eyes.• Follow general directions to complete post card. • Using black floss, buttonhole stitch around edge of post card.

Blessings to Ewe

See pages 23 for CRAZY QUILT basic supplies & assembly.
ADDITIONAL SUPPLIES: 4" x 6" of Tan wool cotton • Wool scraps (Black, White) • Scraps of Green cottons • Embroidery floss (White, Black)
INSTRUCTIONS: Cut a 4" x 6" piece from background fabric. • Print words on fabric sheet. Pattern shown is printed with Baskerville Old Face, size 36 bold. • Trace oval onto Steam-A-Seam 2. Roughly cut around line and remove back-ing. Finger press to back of words. Cut on line and remove backing. • IN REVERSE, trace sheep and hills on Steam-A-Seam 2. Roughly cut around lines and remove backing. Finger press to back of fabrics. Cut on lines and remove backing. Position pieces on background and press. • With white floss, make a French knot for eye. With black floss, make a long stitch where front legs and back legs meet body. • Follow general directions to complete post card. • Buttonhole stitch around post card using black floss.

All My Wishes

See page 23 for QUILT basic supplies & assembly.
ADDITIONAL SUPPLIES: 4" x 6" gold print • Scraps (Gray, White, Black, Red ticking, Gold fabric) • Black embroidery floss
INSTRUCTIONS: Cut a 4" x 6" piece from background fabric. • Print words on fabric. Pattern was printed in Harrington, size 18 bold. • IN REVERSE, trace words piece on Steam-A-Seam 2. Roughly cut around lines and remove back-ing. Finger press to back of words. Cut on lines and remove backing. Position on background and iron. • IN REVERSE, trace cat, wings, star, bird-house, hole, and roof on Steam-A-Seam 2. Roughly cut around lines and remove backing. Finger press to back of fabrics. Cut on lines and remove backings. Position pieces on background and iron. • With black floss buttonhole stitch around birdhouse. Make a few straight stitches around star, backstitch whiskers, and make two French knots for eyes. • Follow general directions to complete card. • Buttonhole stitch around edge with floss.

It's Not Easy Being Queen

See page 23 for QUILT basic supplies & assembly.
ADDITIONAL SUPPLIES: 4" x 6" of gold wool or cotton • Scraps (Rust or Brown wool, printed fabric, Purple tapestry print) • Embroidery floss (Black, Gold)
INSTRUCTIONS: Cut 4" x 6" background fabric. • Print words on fabric. Pattern is printed in American Uncial, size 36 bold italic. • Trace a 6" x 1¼" piece on Steam-A-Seam 2. Roughly cut around line. Remove backing. Finger press to back of words. Cut on line and remove backing. Position on background and iron. • IN REVERSE, trace head, body, collar, and rug on Steam-A-Seam 2. Roughly cut around lines and remove backing. Finger press to back of fabrics. Cut on lines and remove backing. • Position pieces on background and iron. • With 1-ply black floss, stitch eyes, nose, backstitch whiskers and "crease" where legs meet body. With 2-ply gold floss, buttonhole stitch around rug. • Follow general directions to complete card. • Buttonhole stitch around card with black floss.

Come Check Out My Stash

See page 22 for PEN STITCH basic supplies & assembly.
ADDITIONAL SUPPLIES: 4" x 6" of Green quilt fabric • Scrap of Cream fabric • Black Micron Pigma Pen, size .03
INSTRUCTIONS: Trace 4" x 6" piece onto Steam-A-Seam 2. Press to back of background and cut out. • Trace words piece onto fusible web and press to cream fabric. Cut out rectangle. Trace "Come check out my stash" onto rectangle using black pen. Remove backing and press on front of background. • Follow general directions to complete card. • Buttonhole stitch or zig-zag around the outer edge.

A Woman's Work

See pages 23 for QUILT basic supplies & assembly.
ADDITIONAL SUPPLIES: 4" x 6" of Pink wool or cotton
• Scraps of cotton (Green, Pink) • Green embroidery floss
INSTRUCTIONS: Cut a 4" x 6" piece from background fabric. • Print words on fabric leaving 4" space between upper and lower lines. Pattern was printed in Raviet, size 18 bold. • Trace scallop piece onto Steam-A-Seam 2. Roughly cut around line and remove backing. Finger press to back of words. Cut on line and remove backing. Position on background and press. • IN REVERSE, trace apron, tie, apron scallops and pocket on Steam-A-Seam 2. Roughly cut around lines and remove backing. Finger press to back of fabrics and cut on traced lines. Remove backings. Position pieces on post card and iron. • Follow general directions to complete post card.
• Buttonhole stitch around post card using green floss.

Best Wishes

See page 23 for QUILT basic supplies & assembly.
ADDITIONAL SUPPLIES: 6" nylon lace • Thread to match lace • 4" x 6" each of Green floral and Cream floral fabric • Pink embroidery floss • 15" Ecru 1/4" ribbon
INSTRUCTIONS: Cut a 4" x 6" piece from background fabric. Trace a 3 1/4" x 6" piece onto Steam-A-Seam 2 and roughly cut out. Remove backing and finger press to back of foreground fabric. Cut out, remove backing and position over background fabric, aligning right sides. • Position lace, tucking edge under foreground. Iron foreground to background. From back side, make stitches along lace edge to secure. • Print words onto fabric. Pattern is printed in Monotype Corsiva, size 36 bold italic. • Trace oval on Steam-A-Seam 2. Roughly cut out, remove backing, and finger press to back of words. Cut on line and remove backing. Position on foreground and press • With 1-ply floss, buttonhole stitch around oval. • Glue a 3 1/2" by 5 1/2" piece of Pellon to back of background. • Make double French knots in oval where indicated. • Tie ribbon in bow and stitch to oval. • Follow general directions to complete post card. • Buttonhole stitch around outer edge with 1-ply floss.

Thank You

See page 22 for PEN STITCH basic supplies & assembly.
ADDITIONAL SUPPLIES: 4" x 6" of print fabric • Muslin scrap
INSTRUCTIONS: Cut a 4" x 6" piece of print fabric.• Trace scalloped piece on Steam-A-Seam 2 and roughly cut out. Remove backing and finger press to back of muslin. Cut on line. Remove backing and press onto background. • Transfer design onto muslin. Trace words, flowers, leaves and stitched outline with Micron Pigma pen. Color or paint as follows: Flower- red; Middle of flower - purple; Center of flower - yellow; Leaves - green. • Follow general directions to complete card. • Zig-zag stitch around outer edge of post card.

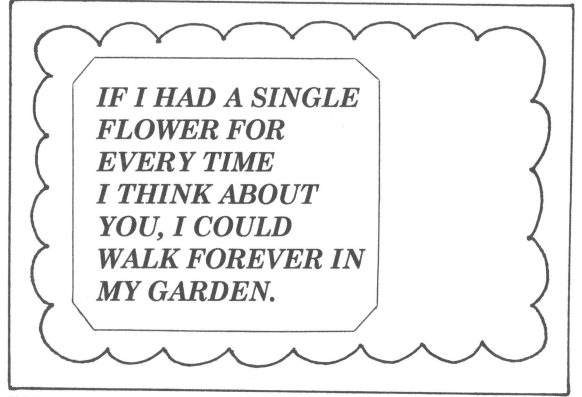

If I Had a Single Flower

See page 23 for QUILT basic supplies & assembly.
ADDITIONAL SUPPLIES: 5" x 7" each of Green cotton and floral with leaves • Gold embroidery floss
INSTRUCTIONS: Cut a 4" x 6" piece from background fabric. • Trace scallops onto Steam-A-Seam 2. Roughly cut around lines and remove backing. Finger press to back of floral fabric. Cut on line and remove backing. Position on background and iron. • Print words onto fabric. Pattern is printed in Century Schoolbook, size 20 bold italic. Trace the words pattern piece onto Steam-A-Seam 2. Roughly cut around line and remove backing. Finger press to back of words. Cut on line and remove backing. Position rectangle onto scalloped floral and iron. • Trace a 2" x 3" piece on Steam-A-Seam 2, cut out, and remove backing. Finger press to back of floral fabric where there is an entire flower and some leaves. Cut around one of the flowers and some leaves or buds. Remove backing, position on right side of post card and iron. • Follow general directions to complete post card. • Buttonhole stitch around post card with gold floss.

The one who dies
with the most fabric
wins

The Most Fabric Wins

See page 22 for PEN STITCH basic supplies & assembly.
ADDITIONAL SUPPLIES: 4" x 6" of Red fabric • Scraps (Cream, Dark Red) • Black Micron Pigma pen, size .03
INSTRUCTIONS: Trace 4" x 6" piece onto Steam-A-Seam 2. Press to background fabric and cut out. • Trace large rectangle onto fusible web, press to red fabric, and cut out. Press to background.• Trace small rectangle onto fusible web, press to cream fabric and cut out. Trace "The one who dies with the most fabric wins" onto rectangle using the Pigma pen. Peel backing off and press to background. • Follow general directions to complete post card. • Buttonhole stitch or zig-zag around outer edge.

With Pins and Needles

See page 22 for PEN STITCH basic supplies & assembly.
ADDITIONAL SUPPLIES: 4" x 6" of novelty print fabric • Scraps of Cream fabric • Black Micron Pigma Pen, size .03
INSTRUCTIONS: Trace 4" x 6" piece onto Steam-A-Seam 2. Remove backing and press to back of background fabric. Cut out. • Trace small rectangle onto fusible web, press to cream fabric and cut out. Trace "With pins and needles" onto rectangle with Black Pigma pen. Remove backing and press to background fabric.• Follow general directions to complete post card. • Buttonhole stitch or zig-zag around outer edge.

With pins
and needles

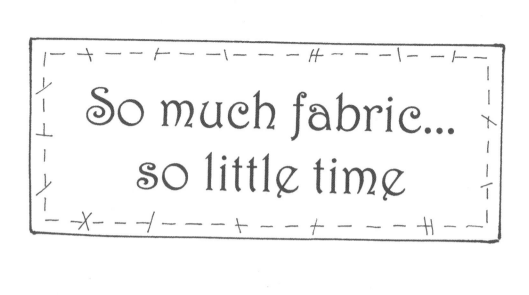

So Much Fabric

See page 22 for PEN STITCH basic supplies & assembly.
ADDITIONAL SUPPLIES: 4" x 6" of brightly colored fabric • Scraps of Cream fabric • Black Micron Pigma Pen, size .03
INSTRUCTIONS: Trace 4" x 6" piece onto Steam-A-Seam 2. Remove backing, press to back of background fabric and cut out. • Trace rectangle onto fusible web, press to cream fabric and cut out. • Trace "So much fabric...so little time" onto cream rectangle using Black Pigma pen. Remove backing and press to front of background fabric.• Follow general directions to complete post card. • Buttonhole stitch or zig-zag around outer edge.

I'd Rather Be Quilting

See pages 22 for PEN STITCH basic supplies & assembly.
ADDITIONAL SUPPLIES: 4" x 6" of thimble print fabric • Scraps of Cream fabric • Black Micron Pigma Pen, size .03
INSTRUCTIONS: Trace 4" x 6" piece onto Steam-A-Seam 2. Remove backing, press to back of background fabric and cut out. • Trace corner pieces onto fusible web, press to cream fabric, and cut out. • Trace oval onto fusible web, press to cream fabric and cut out. Trace "I'd rather be quilting!" onto oval using the Black Pigma pen. Remove backing and press to background. • Follow general directions to complete post card. • Buttonhole stitch or zig-zag around outer edge.

If Friends Were Flowers

See page 23 for QUILT basic supplies & assembly.
ADDITIONAL SUPPLIES: 4" x 6" each of Green cotton and Blue fabric • Scraps (Brown print, floral) • Black embroidery floss
INSTRUCTIONS: Cut a 4" x 6" piece from background fabric. • Trace a $3^1/4$" x $5^1/4$" piece on Steam-A-Seam 2. Roughly cut around lines and remove backing. Finger press to back of blue fabric. Cut on lines and remove backing. Position on background and iron. • Print words on fabric. Pattern was printed in Lucida Calligraphy, size 24 bold italic. Trace words piece on Steam-A-Seam 2. Roughly cut around lines and remove backing. Finger press to back of words.

Cut on line and remove backing. Position on blue background. • Trace basket and handle on Steam-A-Seam 2. Roughly cut around lines and remove backing. Finger press to back of brown print and cut out. Remove backings and position on blue background. • Cut three 2" squares of Steam-A-Seam 2 and remove backing. Finger press to back of flowers/leaves on floral fabric scraps. Cut out 3 motifs and remove backing. Position around basket handles. Press with iron to secure. • With 2-ply black embroidery floss, buttonhole stitch around basket. • Follow general directions to complete post card. • Buttonhole stitch around edge with black floss.

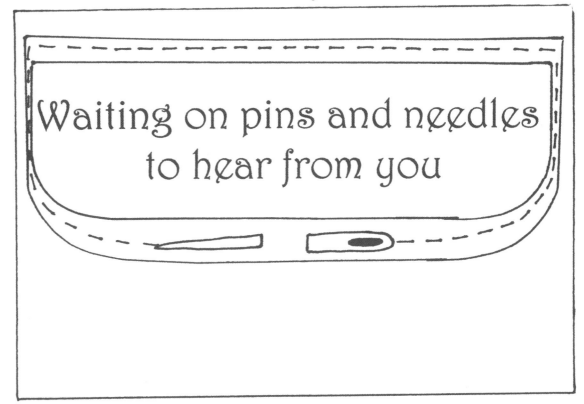

Waiting on Pins

See page 22 for PEN STITCH basic supplies & assembly.
ADDITIONAL SUPPLIES: 4" x 6" of pins and needles print • Scraps (White, Cream, Black) • Black Micron Pigma Pen, size .03
INSTRUCTIONS: Trace 4" x 6" piece onto Steam-A-Seam 2. Remove backing and press to back of background fabric and cut out. • Trace

large flap onto fusible web, press to white fabric, and cut out. Trace small flap onto fusible web, press to cream fabric and cut out. • Trace needle onto fusible web, press to black fabric, and cut out. • Trace "Waiting on pins and needles to hear from you" onto small flap using Pigma pen. Remove backing and press all pieces to background. • Follow general directions to complete post card. • Buttonhole stitch or zig-zag around outer edge.

Bee Happy

See pages 22 for PEN STITCH basic supplies & assembly.
ADDITIONAL SUPPLIES: 4" x 6" of background fabric • Muslin scrap • Micron Pigma pen
INSTRUCTIONS: Trace 4" x 6" piece onto Steam-A-Seam 2. Remove backing, press to back of background fabric and cut out. • Trace scalloped piece onto Steam A Seam 2, cut around lines, remove backing and finger press to muslin scrap. Trace flowers, bee, stitching lines and "Bee Happy" onto piece with Pigma pen. Paint or color the design area. Color guide: Flowers-red; Flower centers-yellow; Leaves-green; Bee-yellow with black stripes. • Follow general directions to complete post card.

Great

See page 22 for PEN STITCH basic supplies & assembly.
ADDITIONAL SUPPLIES: 4" x 6" of scissor print fabric • Scraps (Red, Green, Cream) • Black Micron Pigma Pen, size .03
INSTRUCTIONS: Trace 4" x 6" piece onto Steam-A-Seam 2. Remove backing, press to back of background fabric and cut out. • Trace heart, leaves and oval onto fusible web. Press heart to red fabric, leaves to green and oval to cream and cut out. Trace "Great to see you again!" onto oval using Black Pigma pen. Remove backings and press all pieces to front of background fabric.• Follow general directions to complete post card. • Buttonhole stitch or zig-zag around outer edge.

Sisters Are Special

See page 22 for PEN STITCH basic supplies & assembly.
ADDITIONAL SUPPLIES: 4" x 6" of fan print fabric • Scraps (Cream, Red) • Black Micron Pigma Pen, size .03
INSTRUCTIONS: Trace 4" x 6" piece onto Steam-A-Seam 2. Remove backing, press to back of background fabric and cut out. • Trace scalloped piece onto fusible web, press to red fabric, and cut out. • Trace small rectangle onto fusible web, press to cream fabric and cut out. Trace "Sisters are special" onto rectangle using Pigma pen. Remove backing and press to background fabric. • Follow general directions to complete post card. • Buttonhole stitch or zig-zag around outer edge.

Feel Better

See page 22 for PEN STITCH basic supplies & assembly.
ADDITIONAL SUPPLIES: 5" x 7" of sunshine print fabric • Scraps (Yellow, Blue, Cream) • Black Micron Pigma Pen, size .03
INSTRUCTIONS: Trace 4" x 6" piece onto Steam-A-Seam 2. Remove backing, press to back of background fabric and cut out. • Trace sun onto fusible web, press to sun on print fabric, and cut out. Trace large rectangle, press to blue fabric, and cut out • Trace curved rectangle onto fusible web, press to cream fabric and cut out. Trace "I hope you feel better soon" onto piece using Pigma pen. Remove backing and press all pieces to background. • Follow general directions to complete post card. • Buttonhole stitch or zig-zag around outer edge.

Life Gives You Scraps

See page 22 for PEN STITCH basic supplies & assembly.
ADDITIONAL SUPPLIES: 4" x 6" of yellow floral fabric • Scraps (Green, Cream) • Black Micron Pigma Pen, size .03 • Yellow 1" button • 2¹/₂" doily
INSTRUCTIONS: Trace 4" x 6" piece onto Steam-A-Seam 2. Press to back of yellow background fabric and cut out. • Trace scalloped rectangle, stem and leaf onto fusible web, cut out, remove backing and press to backs of fabrics as follows: leaf & stem to green fabric, scalloped rectangle to cream fabric. Cut pieces out. • Trace "When life gives you scraps, make a quilt" onto rectangle using Pigma pen. Remove backing and press to background. • Remove backings and press stem and leaf to right side of words. • Sew doily to top of stem and add button.• Follow general directions to complete post card. •. Buttonhole stitch or zig-zag around outer edge.

#1 Teacher

See page 22 for PEN STITCH basic supplies & assembly.
ADDITIONAL SUPPLIES: 4" x 6" of print fabric • Scraps (Muslin, Green) • Black Micron Pigma Pen, size .03
INSTRUCTIONS: Trace 4" x 6" piece onto Steam-A-Seam 2. Press to back of background fabric and cut out. • Trace small rectangle, apple, and leaves onto fusible web, cut out, remove backing and press to backs of fabrics as follows: leaves to green fabric, apple to background fabric, rectangle to muslin. Cut pieces out. • Trace "#1 Teacher" onto rectangle using Black Pigma pen. Remove backing and press to background. • Remove backings and press apple and leaves to left side of words. Add stitching line, stem and leaf details with pen.• Follow general directions to complete post card. • Buttonhole stitch or zig-zag around outer edge.

In the crazy quilt of life,
I'm glad you're in
my block of friends.

Crazy Quilt of Life

See page 22 for PEN STITCH basic supplies & assembly.
ADDITIONAL SUPPLIES: 4" x 6" of spool fabric • Scraps (Pink, Cream) • Black Micron Pigma Pen, size .03
INSTRUCTIONS: Trace 4" x 6" piece onto Steam-A-Seam 2. Press to back of spool fabric and cut out. • Trace both rectangles onto fusible web. Cut out, remove backing, and press to fabrics as follows: large rectangle to pink fabric, small rectangle to cream fabric. Cut pieces out. • Trace "In the crazy quilt of life, I'm glad you're in my block of friends" onto cream rectangle using Black Pigma pen. Remove backings and press pieces together. • Follow general directions to complete post card. • Buttonhole stitch or zig-zag around outer edge.

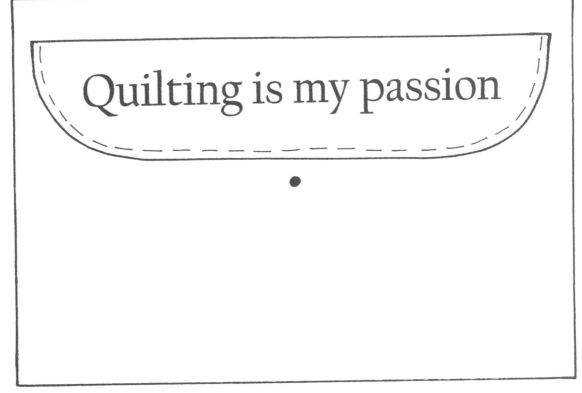

Quilting is my passion

Quilting is My Passion

See page 22 for PEN STITCH basic supplies & assembly.
ADDITIONAL SUPPLIES: 4" x 6" of floral fabric • Scraps of Cream fabric • Black Micron Pigma Pen, size .03 • Pink 3/4" button
INSTRUCTIONS: Trace 4" x 6" piece onto Steam-A-Seam 2. Remove backing, press to back of background fabric and cut out. • Trace flap onto fusible web, press to cream fabric and cut out. Trace "Quilting is my passion" onto flap piece using black Pigma pen. Remove backing and press to background fabric. • Sew a pink button on front. • Follow general directions to complete post card. • Buttonhole stitch or zig-zag around outer edge.

YOU ARE MY SUNSHINE

You Are My Sunshine

See page 23 for QUILT basic supplies & assembly.
ADDITIONAL SUPPLIES: 4" x 6" each of Purple cotton and Golden cotton • Scraps (two colors Purple, Black, Muslin) • Embroidery floss (Golden, Pink, Green)
INSTRUCTIONS: Cut a 4" x 6" piece from background fabric. • Trace a 3³/₈" x 5¹/₄" rectangle on Steam-A-Seam 2. Roughly cut around lines and remove backing. Finger press to back of Golden fabric. Cut on lines and remove backing. Position on background and iron. • IN REVERSE, trace dress, dress sleeve, pinafore, bonnet, shoes, and hand on Steam-A-Seam 2. Roughly cut around traced lines and remove backing. Finger press pieces to fabrics. Cut on lines and remove backing. Position pieces on background and press. • With 1-ply golden floss, buttonhole stitch around bonnet. With 2-ply green floss, make stitches for stems. With 2-ply pink floss, make French knots for flowers. • Print words on fabric. Pattern was printed in Lucida Calligraphy, size 28 bold. Trace words piece on Steam-A-Seam 2. Roughly cut around line and remove backing. Position on back of words, cut on line and remove backing. Position words and iron. • Follow general directions to complete post card. • Buttonhole stitch around edge with 1-ply floss.

Quilting With a Friend

See page 22 for PEN STITCH basic supplies & assembly.
ADDITIONAL SUPPLIES: 4" x 6" quilt fabric • Scraps (Pink, Cream) • Black Micron Pigma Pen, size .03 • Pink 1" button
INSTRUCTIONS: Trace 4" x 6" piece onto Steam-A-Seam 2. Press to back of background fabric and cut out. • Trace both rectangles and heart onto fusible web. Cut pieces out, remove backing, and press to backs of fabrics as follows: large rectangle and heart to pink, small rectangle to cream. Cut pieces out. • Trace "Quilting with a friend will keep you in stitches" onto cream rectangle using black Pigma pen. Remove backing and press to pink rectangle. Remove backing from pink rectangle, position on background and press. • Remove backing from heart and press to background. Sew pink button on heart. • Follow general directions to complete post card. • Buttonhole stitch or zig-zag around outer edge.

Quilting with a friend will keep you in stitches

Friends Are the Fabric of Life

See pages 22 for PEN STITCH basic supplies & assembly.
ADDITIONAL SUPPLIES: 4" x 6" of Purple floral • Scraps (Pink, Gold, Cream, Green) • Black Micron Pigma Pen, size .03
INSTRUCTIONS: Trace 4" x 6" piece onto Steam-A-Seam 2. Press to back of purple floral and cut out. • Trace rectangle, flower, center, leaf, and stem onto fusible web. Cut out, remove backing and press to backs of fabrics as follows: flower to pink, center to gold, leaf and stem to green, rectangle to cream. Cut pieces out. • Trace "Friends are the fabric of life" onto rectangle using Pigma pen. Remove backing and press on the front of purple fabric. • Attach leaf and stem, flower and center. • Follow general directions to complete post card. • Buttonhole stitch or zig-zag around outer edge.

Best Friend

See page 22 for PEN STITCH basic supplies & assembly.
ADDITIONAL SUPPLIES: 4" x 6" of Purple fabric • Scraps (Gold, Floral, Green, Cream) • Black Micron Pigma Pen, size .03
INSTRUCTIONS: Trace 4" x 6" piece onto Steam-A-Seam 2. Remove backing, press to back of background fabric and cut out. • Trace flowers, centers, leaves, stems and rectangle onto fusible web. Press to fabrics as follows: flowers to floral, centers to gold, leaves and stems to green, and rectangle to cream. Cut out all pieces. • Trace "You're my best friend" onto rectangle using Pigma pen. Remove backings and press all pieces to background. • Follow general directions to complete post card. • Buttonhole stitch or zig-zag around outer edge.

Think Spring

See page 23 for QUILT basic supplies & assembly.

ADDITIONAL SUPPLIES: 4" x 6" of Pink felt, wool or cotton • 5" square Off-White fabric • Scraps of floral fabric • Embroidery floss (Pink, Gold)

INSTRUCTIONS: Cut 4" x 6" piece of pink felt. • Print words on fabric sheet. Pattern was printed in Andy, size 36 bold italic. Trace words piece on Steam-A-Seam 2. Roughly cut around line and remove backing. Finger press to back of words. Cut on line and remove backing. Position words on background. • IN REVERSE, trace rabbit on Steam-A-Seam 2. Roughly cut around lines and remove backing. Finger press to back of off-white fabric. Cut on lines and remove backing. Position on background. • Cut two 2¹/₂" squares of Steam-a-Seam 2 and remove backing. Finger press to back of floral fabric. Cut out flowers/leaves/stems and remove backings. Position on post card and press all pieces. • With 1-ply pink floss, backstitch between ears, between legs, chin, and at haunches. Make small stitches for nose and a double French knot for eye. • Follow general directions to complete post card. • Buttonhole stitch around card using 2-ply gold floss.

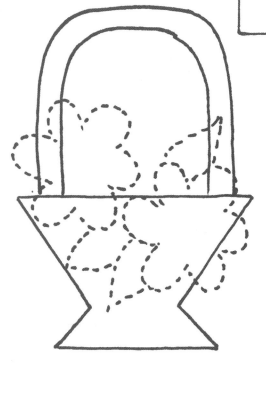

Basket of Flowers

See page 24 for WOOL basic supplies & assembly.

ADDITIONAL SUPPLIES: 4" x 6" of Gray-Green wool • Wool scraps (Brown, Green, Yellow, Lilac) • Embroidery floss (Purple, Green, Yellow, White)

INSTRUCTIONS: Cut 4" x 6" piece from gray-green wool. • Trace basket, flowers and leaves on Steam-A-Seam 2. Cut around lines and remove backings. Finger press to backs of scrap wool, cut out, remove backings and press to card. • With 6-ply floss, make 3 French knots in the center of each flower, using purple and yellow. With 2-ply floss, make straight stitches coming from center of each flower. • Follow general directions to complete post card. • Edge post card with blanket stitch using 6-ply blue floss.

Rabbit With Flower

See page 24 for WOOL basic supplies & assembly.
ADDITIONAL SUPPLIES: 4" x 6" of Blue-Violet wool • Wool scraps (Tan, Coral, Yellow, Green) • Embroidery floss (Green, Yellow, Tan, Black)
INSTRUCTIONS: Cut a 4" x 6" piece of Blue-Violet wool. • Trace rabbit, arm, leg, flower, center and leaves onto Steam-A-Seam 2. Cut around lines and remove backing. Finger press to wool scraps, cut out, remove backings, and press to background. • With 2-ply green floss stitch veins in leaves. With tan floss, blanket stitch around rabbit, including leg and arm pieces. With 4-ply yellow floss, make 5 French knots in center of flower. With 2-ply black floss make French knot for eye. • Follow general directions to complete post card. • Edge card with a zig-zag stitch.

Chick & Egg

See page 24 for WOOL basic supplies & assembly.
ADDITIONAL SUPPLIES: 4" x 6" of Coral wool • Wool scraps (White, Pale Yellow, Blue, Green) • Pearl cotton (Green, Yellow, Cream) • Embroidery floss (Black, Yellow)
INSTRUCTIONS: Cut a 4" x 6" piece of coral wool. • Trace bird, wing, egg, flower, center and leaves on Steam-A-Seam 2. Cut around all pieces, remove backings, and finger press to wool scraps. Cut out and remove backings. Position on background and press. • Blanket stitch around egg with green pearl cotton, and around chick with cream. Straight stitch around wing with cream pearl cotton. Make 5 French knots in center of flower with 4-ply yellow floss. Use 2-ply black floss to make French knot for eye. • Follow general directions to complete post card. • Edge with blanket stitch, using yellow pearl cotton.

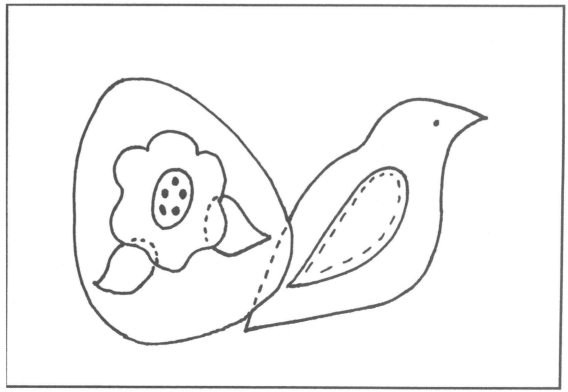

Friends

See page 23 for QUILT basic supplies & assembly.
ADDITIONAL SUPPLIES: 4" x 6" each of Pink floral and Black print fabric • 5" square scrap of Pink wool or cotton • Scrap of Light Pink print • Black embroidery floss • Quilt marking pencil
INSTRUCTIONS: Cut a 4" x 6" piece from pink floral fabric. • Trace a $3^{1}/4$" x $5^{1}/4$" piece on Steam-A-Seam 2. Roughly cut around lines and remove backing. Finger press to back of black print. Cut on lines. Remove backing. Position on background and press. • IN REVERSE, trace band and heart on Steam-A-Seam 2. Cut roughly around lines and remove backing. Finger press to back of fabrics. Cut on lines. • Using quilt marking pencil, trace "FRIENDS" on fabric. Remove backing and position across heart. Trim edges. Remove backing from heart piece and position on post card. Press heart and band. • Using 2-ply black floss, backstitch "FRIENDS". Buttonhole stitch around edge of heart. • Follow general directions to complete card. • Buttonhole stitch around post card black floss.

Lace, Doily & Button Flower

See page 23 for QUILT basic supplies & assembly.
ADDITIONAL SUPPLIES: 4" x 6" of print fabric • Scraps of Green fabric • 7" of $2^{1}/2$" lace • Doily • Button
INSTRUCTIONS: Cut a 4" x 6" piece from background fabric. • Trace leaves on Steam-A-Seam 2. Cut around lines and remove backings. Finger press to back of green scraps and cut on lines. • Trace lace and doily on Steam-A-Seam 2. Cut out on lines and remove backings. Press to pieces. • Remove backings from lace, doily and leaves, position on background and press. • Sew button to center of doily. • Follow general directions to complete post card. • Zig-zag around edge of post card.

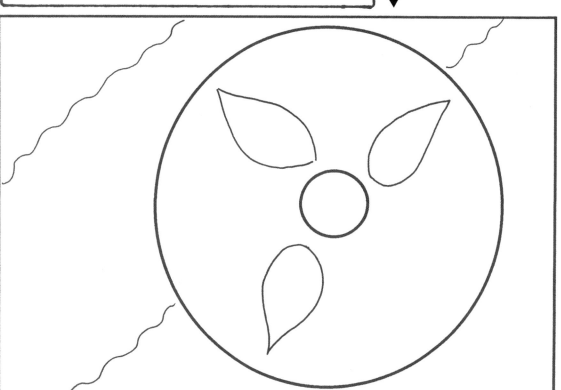

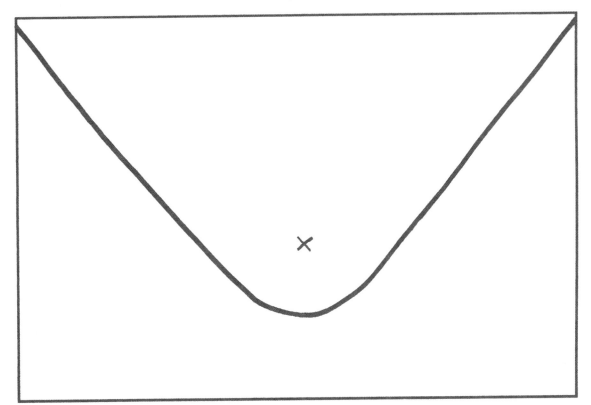

Envelope With Button ▲

See page 23 for QUILT basic supplies & assembly.
ADDITIONAL SUPPLIES: 4" x 6" of print fabric • Scrap of coordinating fabric • ³/₄" button
INSTRUCTIONS: Cut a 4" x 6" piece of background fabric. • Trace flap onto Steam-A-Seam 2. Cut out around lines and remove backing. Finger press to back of coordinating fabric. Remove backing and press to background. Stitch button to flap. • Follow general directions to complete post card. • Zig-zag stitch around edge of post card.

The Best Antique is an Old Friend ▶

See page 23 for QUILT basic supplies & assembly.
ADDITIONAL SUPPLIES: 4" x 9" of antique looking fabric • Scraps (Pink, Cream plaid • 2" of 1³/₈" lace • Thread to match lace • Vintage button • Embroidery floss (Pink, Blue)
INSTRUCTIONS: Cut 4" x 6" piece from background fabric. • Print words on fabric. Pattern was printed in Perpetua, size 24 bold italic. • Trace oval on Steam-A-Seam 2. Roughly cut around line and remove backing. Finger press to back of words. Cut on line and remove backing. Position on background. • Trace both scallops on Steam-A-Seam 2. Roughly cut around lines and remove backing. Finger press to back of fabrics. Cut out and remove backings. Position on background. • Position lace, tucking ends under scallops and words. Iron all pieces in place. From the back, make a few stitches to secure lace to background. • Sew button on scallops. • With 1-ply pink floss, buttonhole stitch around oval. • Follow general directions to complete post card. • Buttonhole stitch around post card with 2-ply blue floss.

Flowers With Leaves on Lace

See page 23 for QUILT basic supplies & assembly.
ADDITIONAL SUPPLIES: 4" x 6" of print fabric • Scraps (Pink, Green) • $5/8$" button
INSTRUCTIONS: Cut a 4" x 6" piece from background fabric. • Trace flower, center and leaves on Steam-A-Seam 2. Cut around lines and remove backings. Finger press to scraps. Cut on lines and remove backings. Position on background and press. • Stitch button to center of flower • Follow general directions to complete post card. • Zig-zag around outer edge of post card.

Wool Pumpkin With Crow

See page 24 for WOOL basic supplies & assembly.
ADDITIONAL SUPPLIES: 4" x 6" of Purple wool • Wool scraps (Orange, Green, Black) • Green embroidery floss • Pearl cotton (Gold, Orange)
INSTRUCTIONS: Cut a 4" x 6" piece from background fabric. • Trace pumpkin, leaves, stem and crow on Steam-A-Seam 2. Roughly cut around lines and remove backing. Finger press to back of scraps. Cut on lines and remove backing. Position and iron. • Blanket stitch around pumpkin using orange pearl cotton. Stitch veins in leaves and vines with 2-ply green floss. Stitch star with gold pearl cotton. • Follow general directions to complete post card. • Blanket stitch around post card with gold pearl cotton.

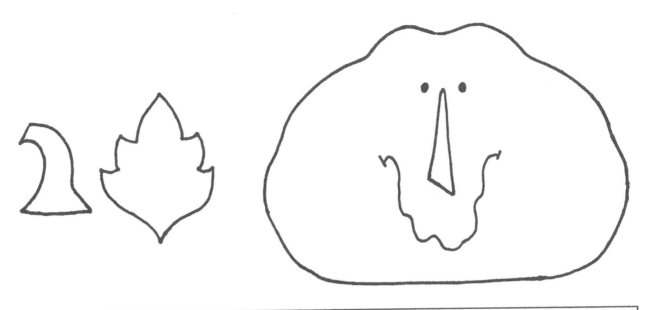

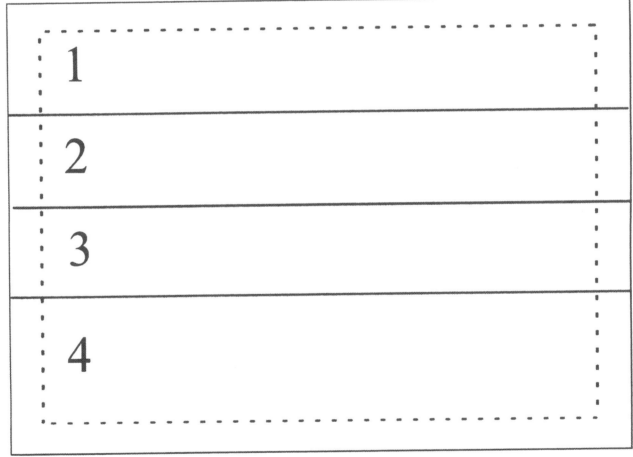

Crazy Quilt With Pumpkin

See page 23 for CRAZY QUILT basic supplies & assembly.
ADDITIONAL SUPPLIES: Four Black print scraps for background • Scraps (Orange print, Black solid, Green print) • Green floss • Black Micron Pigma Pen • Orange thread
INSTRUCTIONS: Cut a 4" x 6" piece of muslin. Cut strips from Steam-A- Steam 2, press to backs of black scraps, and cut out. Press to background. Zig-zag along edges of strips. • Cut pumpkin, leaf, stem and nose from Steam-A-Seam 2. Remove backings and press to back side of scraps. Cut out on lines. Position on card and press. Zig-zag around edges and sides of pumpkin. • Trace eyes and nose with black pen. • Stitch veins and stem with 2-ply green floss. • Follow general directions to complete post card. • Zig-zag around edge with orange thread.

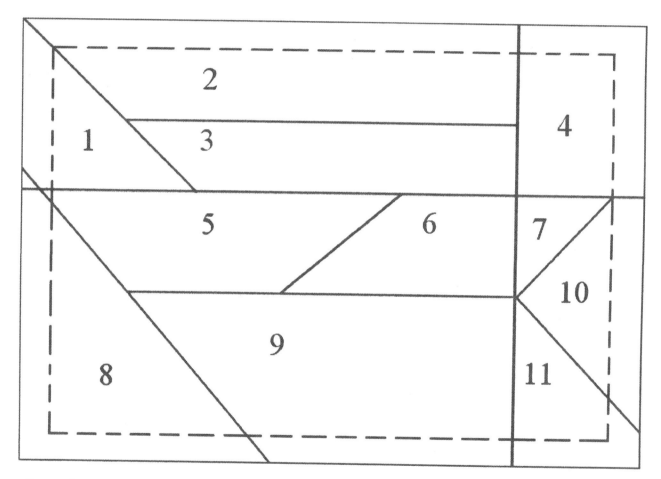

Crazy Quilt With Crow

See page 23 for CRAZY QUILT basic supplies & assembly.
ADDITIONAL SUPPLIES: Scraps (11 pieces in fall colors, Black, Gold)
• Black floss • Orange thread

INSTRUCTIONS: Cut a 4" x 6" piece of muslin. Trace background pieces onto Steam-A-Seam 2. Cut out and apply to back of scraps. Cut pieces on lines and press to background. Zig-zag edges. • Cut crow and star from Steam-A-Seam 2. Press to scraps, remove backing and press to background. • Stitch legs with 2-ply black floss. • Follow general directions to complete post card. • Zig-zag around outer edge.

Wool Turkey

See page 24 for WOOL basic supplies & assembly.
ADDITIONAL SUPPLIES: 4" x 6" of Black wool • Wool scraps (5 colors for feathers, Brown for wings, Red for wattle, Gold for beak) • Orange Pearl cotton • Embroidery floss (Gold, Black)
INSTRUCTIONS: Cut a 4" x 6" piece of background fabric. • Trace feathers, turkey, wings, wattle and beak onto Steam-A-Seam 2, cut around lines, and remove backings. Finger press to scraps and cut out. Position on background and press. • With 2-ply gold floss, stitch legs and V shapes on body. With 1-ply black floss, stitch nose and make French knots for eyes. • Follow general directions to complete post card. • Blanket stitch around outer edge with orange pearl cotton.

Wool Pumpkin

See page 24 for WOOL basic supplies & assembly.
ADDITIONAL SUPPLIES: 4" x 6" of Black wool • Wool scraps (Orange, Rust, Gold, Green, Black) • Embroidery floss (Gold, Green, Rust, Black) • Gold thread
INSTRUCTIONS: Cut a 4" x 6" piece of black wool • Trace pumpkin, nose, leaves and stem onto Steam-A-Seam 2, cut around lines and remove backings. Finger press to scraps, remove backings, position on post card and press. • With 2-ply floss, stitch veins, vine, eyes and mouth, and make French knots.• Follow general directions to complete post card. • Zig-zag stitch around outer edge.

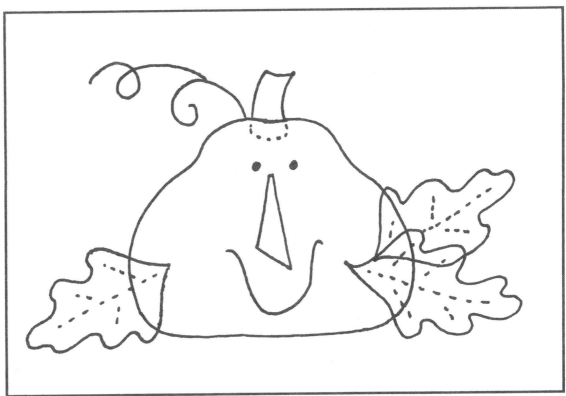

Have Time to Stitch?

See page 22 for PEN STITCH basic supplies & assembly.
ADDITIONAL SUPPLIES: 4" x 6" of Fall fabric • Scraps (Cream, Gold) • Black Micron Pigma Pen, size .03
INSTRUCTIONS: Trace 4" x 6" piece onto Steam-A-Seam 2. Remove backing, press to back of background fabric and cut out. • Trace curved piece and rectangle onto fusible web, press to fabrics, and cut out. Trace "Have time to stitch?" onto cream rectangle using the Pigma pen. Remove backing and press to curved piece. Remove backing from curved piece and press to background • Follow general directions to complete post card. • Buttonhole stitch or zig-zag around outer edge.

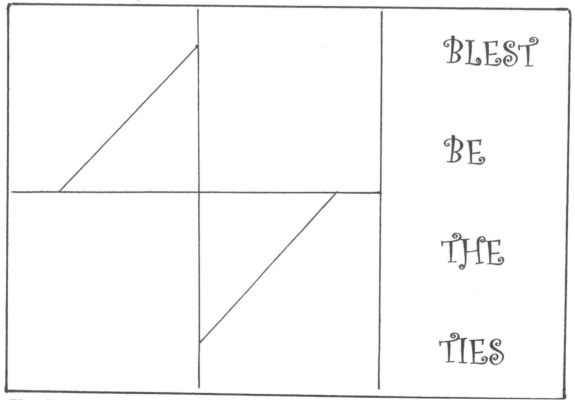

Blest Be the Ties

See page 23 for QUILT basic supplies & assembly.
ADDITIONAL SUPPLIES: Scraps (Brown print, Gold print) • Black embroidery floss • Quilt marking pencil
INSTRUCTIONS: Print words on fabric sheet. Pattern is printed in Curlz MT, size 28 bold, and fits in a 2" x 4" space. Trace a 4" x 6" piece with words on right side. Cut out. • Trace a 4" x 4" square on Steam-A-Seam 2. Roughly cut around lines and remove backing. Finger press to back of gold print fabric. Cut out and remove backing. Position on background and press.• Trace two 2" x 2" squares on Steam-A-Seam 2. Roughly cut around lines and remove backing. Finger press to back of brown print. Cut on lines and remove backing. Position in opposite corners. • Trace a 1$\frac{1}{2}$" x 1$\frac{1}{2}$" square on Steam-A-Seam 2. Finger press to back of brown print. Cut on lines, then cut square in half diagonally. Remove backing. • Position triangles over gold print fabric. Iron all pieces in place. • Follow general directions to complete post card. • Buttonhole stitch around post card edge with black floss.

Let's Trade Buttons

See page 22 for PEN STITCH basic supplies & assembly.
ADDITIONAL SUPPLIES: 4" x 6" of button print • Cream fabric scraps • Black Micron Pigma Pen, size .03 • Blue 3/4" button
INSTRUCTIONS: Trace 4" x 6" piece onto Steam-A-Seam 2. Remove backing and press to back of background and cut out. • Trace flap onto fusible web, press to cream fabric and cut out. Trace "Let's trade buttons" onto flap using Pigma pen. Remove backing and press to background. • Sew button to flap. • Follow general directions to complete post card. • Buttonhole stitch or zig-zag around outer edge.

Creative Minds

See page 22 for PEN STITCH basic supplies & assembly.
ADDITIONAL SUPPLIES: 4" x 6" of spool print fabric • Fabric scraps (Cream, Gold, Pink, Blue) • Black Micron Pigma Pen, size .03
INSTRUCTIONS: Trace 4" x 6" piece onto Steam-A-Seam 2. Remove backing and press to back of background fabric and cut out. • Trace spools and thread onto fusible web, press to scraps, and cut out. • Trace word piece onto fusible web, press to cream fabric and cut out. Trace "Creative minds are rarely tidy" onto piece using black Pigma pen. Remove backing and press to background. • Follow general directions to complete post card. • Buttonhole stitch or zig-zag around outer edge.

Thanks For Everything

See page 22 for PEN STITCH basic supplies & assembly.
ADDITIONAL SUPPLIES: 4" x 6" of shell fabric • Fabric scraps (Cream, Tan) • Black Micron Pigma Pen, size .03 • 1 1/2" Doily
INSTRUCTIONS: Trace 4" x 6" piece onto Steam-A-Seam 2. Remove backing, press to back of background fabric and cut out. • Trace flap onto fusible web, press to tan fabric, and cut out. • Trace oval onto fusible web, press to cream fabric, and cut out. Trace "Thanks for everything" onto oval using black Pigma pen. Remove backing and press to flap. Remove backing from flap and press to background. • Sew doily to front. • Follow general directions to complete post card. • Buttonhole stitch or zig-zag around outer edge.

Quilters Aren't Greedy

See page 22 for PEN STITCH basic supplies & assembly.
ADDITIONAL SUPPLIES: 4" x 6" of background fabric • Fabric scraps (Gold, Red) • Black Micron Pigma Pen, size .03
INSTRUCTIONS: Trace 4" x 6" piece onto Steam-A-Seam 2. Remove backing, press to back of background fabric and cut out. • Trace large rectangle onto fusible web. Press to gold fabric and cut out. • Trace small rectangle onto fusible web, press to cream fabric, and cut out. Trace "Quilters aren't greedy, They're just materialistic!" onto small rectangle using black Pigma pen. • Trace flowers onto fusible web, press to red and gold fabrics, and cut out. Remove backing and press to background. • Follow general directions to complete post card. • Buttonhole stitch or zig-zag around outer edge of post card.

Stars

See page 23 for QUILT basic supplies & assembly.
ADDITIONAL SUPPLIES: 4" x 6" of printed cotton • Gold fabric scraps
• Five 1/2" buttons
INSTRUCTIONS: Trace 4" x 6" piece onto Steam-A-Seam 2. Remove back-ing, press to back of background and cut out. • Transfer stars to fusible web, press to scraps, and cut out. Position on background and press. • Stitch buttons to stars. • Follow general directions to complete post card. • Buttonhole stitch or zig-zag around outer edge.

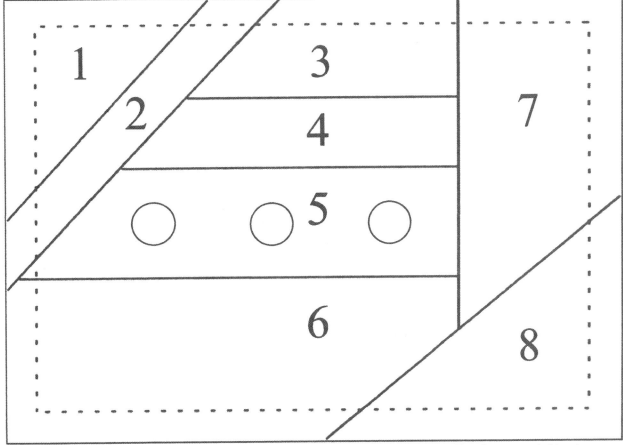

Fall Crazy Quilt

See page 23 for QUILT basic supplies & assembly.
ADDITIONAL SUPPLIES: Scraps of 8 different fabrics • Three 1/2" buttons
INSTRUCTIONS: Trace 4" x 6" piece onto Steam-A-Seam 2. Remove backing, press to muslin and cut out. • Trace 8 pieces onto fusible web, press to scraps and cut out. Remove backing and press to background. Zig-zag over edges. • Sew buttons to card. • Follow general directions to complete post card. • Buttonhole stitch or zig-zag around outer edge.

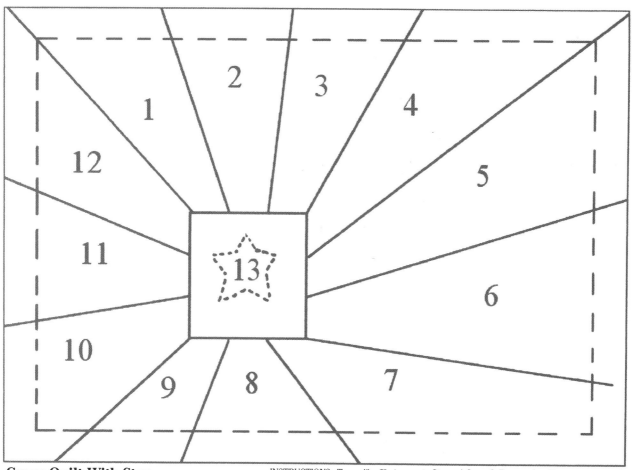

Crazy Quilt With Star

See page 23 for QUILT basic supplies & assembly.
ADDITIONAL SUPPLIES: Scraps of 13 fabrics • ³/4" star button

INSTRUCTIONS: Trace 4" x 6" piece onto Steam-A-Seam 2. Remove backing, press to muslin and cut out. • Trace 13 pieces onto fusible web, press to scraps and cut out. Remove backing and press to background. Zig-zag edges. • Sew button to card. • Follow general directions to complete post card. • Buttonhole stitch or zig-zag around outer edge.

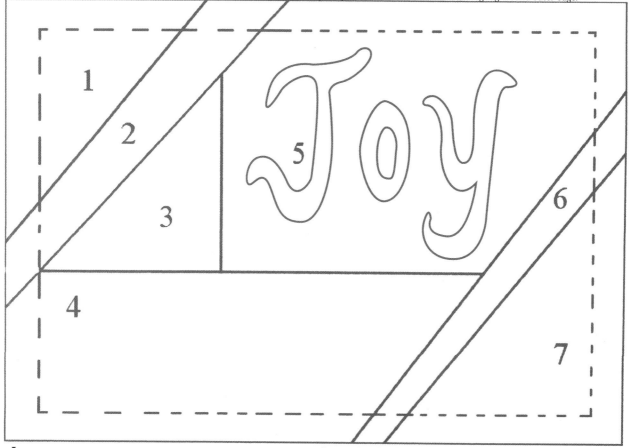

Joy

See page 23 for QUILT basic supplies & assembly.
ADDITIONAL SUPPLIES: Scraps of 7 fabrics • Two ¹/2" star buttons. •

Green embroidery floss
INSTRUCTIONS: Trace 4" x 6" piece onto Steam-A-Seam 2. Remove backing, press to muslin and cut out. • Trace 7 pieces onto fusible web, press to scraps and cut out. Remove backing and press to background. Zig-zag edges. • Stitch "Joy" with 2-ply green floss. • Sew buttons to card. • Follow general directions to complete post card. Buttonhole stitch or zig-zag around outer edge.

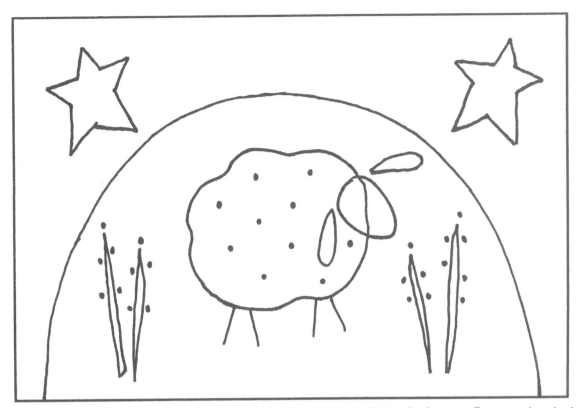

Wool Sheep

See page 24 for WOOL basic supplies & assembly.
ADDITIONAL SUPPLIES: 4" x 6" of Black wool • Wool scraps (Gold, Off-White, Black, Blue, Green) • Embroidery floss (White, Yellow, Black) • Blue pearl cotton • Two 3/8" gold buttons
INSTRUCTIONS: Trace 4" x 6" piece onto Steam-A-Seam 2. Remove backing, press to black wool and cut out. • Trace stars, sheep, head, ears, hill and stems onto fusible web, press to scraps and cut out. Remove backings and press to background. • Blanket stitch around hill using blue pearl cotton. Make French knots for sheep curls using 6-ply white floss. Make French knots for flowers using 4-ply yellow floss. Use 2-ply black floss for sheep legs. • Stitch buttons to stars. • Follow general directions to complete post card. • Zig-zag around outer edge.

The Promise of the Christmas Star

See page 23 for QUILT basic supplies & assembly.
ADDITIONAL SUPPLIES: 4" x 6" of Black wool or cotton • Scraps (Off-White wool, Brown, Gold, Green print) • Pearl cotton (Cream, Red)
INSTRUCTIONS: Cut a 4" x 6" piece from background fabric. • Print words on fabric. Pattern was printed in Abadi MT Condensed, size 18 bold. Trace words pattern on Steam-A-Seam 2. Roughly cut around lines and remove backing. Finger press piece to back of words. Cut out and remove backing. Position on right side of post card. • IN REVERSE, trace snow, tree trunk, tree, and star on Steam-A-Seam 2. Roughly cut around lines and remove backings. Finger press pieces to back of scraps. Cut out and remove backings. Position on background fabric and press. • With cream pearl cotton, make straight stitches around star. With red pearl cotton, make French knots at ends of tree branches. • Follow general directions to complete post card. • Buttonhole stitch around outer edge with cream pearl cotton.

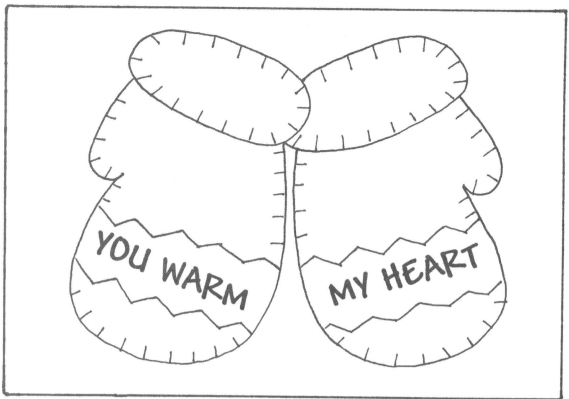

You Warm My Heart

See page 23 for QUILT basic supplies & assembly.
ADDITIONAL SUPPLIES: 4" x 6" each of Red print and Black/White check • Scraps of Black wool or cotton • Off-White embroidery floss
INSTRUCTIONS: Cut 4" x 6" piece from background fabric. • Trace mittens and cuffs on Steam-A-Seam 2. Roughly cut out and remove backing. Finger press to back of fabrics. Cut out and remove back-ings. Position on background and press. • Print words on fabric. Pattern was printed in Andy, size 28 bold. Trace words pieces onto Steam-A-Seam 2. Roughly cut around traced lines. Finger press to the back of words. Cut out and remove backings. Position on each mitten and press. • With 2-ply off-white floss, buttonhole stitch around mittens and cuffs. Tie bows of floss on cuffs. • Follow general directions to complete post card. • Buttonhole stitch around post card with 2-ply floss.

Wool Gingerbread

See page 24 for WOOL basic supplies & assembly.
ADDITIONAL SUPPLIES: 4" x 6" of Black wool • Wool scraps (Rust, Green) • Embroidery floss (White, Green, Red, Black) • Red Pearl cotton
INSTRUCTIONS: Cut 4" x 6" piece from background fabric. • Trace gingerbread man and leaves on Steam-A-Seam 2. Roughly cut out and remove backings. Finger press to back of scraps. Cut out and remove backings. Position on background and press. • With 2-ply green floss, stitch veins on leaves. With 2-ply red floss, stitch Xs on man and with 6-ply, make French knots for berries. With 6-ply white floss, make French knots around edge of man. With 2-ply black floss, make French knots for eyes. • Follow general directions to complete post card. • Buttonhole stitch around post card with red pearl cotton.

Winter Sampler

See page 22 for PEN STITCH basic supplies & assembly.
ADDITIONAL SUPPLIES: Muslin • Glitter or Diamond Dust • White paint • Black Micron Pigma Pen
INSTRUCTIONS: Cut a 4" x 6" piece of muslin.• Transfer design onto muslin. Trace with Micron Pigma pen. Color or paint as follows: Mittens - green, red, white; Snowmen - white, orange, black; Star with leaves - gold, green; Joy - red. • Follow general directions to complete post card. • Add glitter or Diamond Dust between horizontal and vertical dashed areas. • Zig zag stitch around outer edge of post card.

Snowman With Tree ▶

See page 22 for PEN STITCH basic supplies & assembly.
ADDITIONAL SUPPLIES: Muslin • White paint • Glitter or Diamond Dust • Black Micron Pigma Pen
INSTRUCTIONS: Cut a 4" x 6" piece of muslin.• Transfer design onto muslin. Trace with Micron Pigma pen. Color or paint as follows: Snowman - white; Nose - orange; Scarf - red; Tree - green; Star - yellow. Add snow to bottom portion of card by dabbing paintbrush in white paint, wiping most of it off, then tapping brush over fabric.
• Add glitter or Diamond Dust to star and all white areas of snowman and snow. • Follow general directions to complete post card.
• Zig zag stitch around outer edge of post card.

Peace Sheep

See page 22 for PEN STITCH basic supplies & assembly.
ADDITIONAL SUPPLIES: Muslin • Glitter or Diamond Dust
• Micron Pigma Pen
INSTRUCTIONS: Cut a 4" x 6" piece of muslin. • Transfer design onto muslin. Trace with Micron Pigma pen. Color or paint as follows: Sheep - white; Head & Ears - black; Trees - green; Stars - yellow. Draw curls on sheep after paint has dried. • Add glitter or Diamond Dust to stars, sheep, ground and down right side of trees. • Follow general directions to complete post card. • Zig zag stitch around outer edge of post card.

Oh Holy Night

See page 21 for PEN STITCH basic supplies & assembly.
ADDITIONAL SUPPLIES: Muslin • Glitter or Diamond Dust • White paint • Micron Pigma Pen
INSTRUCTIONS: Cut a 4" x 6" piece of muslin. • Transfer design onto muslin. Trace with Micron Pigma pen. Color or paint as follows: Large snowman - green hat, brown coat; Small snowman - green coat, red hat and cuff; Snowmen, tassels, cuffs - white; Star - gold. • Add glitter or Diamond Dust to star and all white portions of snowmen and clothing. • Follow general directions to complete post card. • Zig zag stitch around outer edge of post card.

Have a great day!

I'm not messy,
I'm creative.

Old quilters never die
They just go to pieces

A fat quarter
is not a body part.

Quilters never cut corners

Stitch your stress away.

Quilting with a friend
will keep you in stitches.

Happy Birthday

Happiness is handmade

Merry Christmas

I've been busting my stitches

Happy New Years

May your sorrows be
patched
and your joys quilted.

We are like sisters

**From your
secret sister**

From one quilter
to another!

*You really know
how to live!*

*Friends are like quilts...
They value with age.*

Post Card

Suzie South
1021 Ranches
Santa Fe, NM

Hello Janie,
  I think of you often and hope we can visit at the "Girls' Reunion" this Fall.
  See you soon.
  Your friend, Suzie

Janie Brown
1809 Elm Crest Drive
Arlington, TX 76012
  U.S.A.

Place a standard postage stamp in place, and send your card right through the mail.

Happy Valentine's Day

Happy Thanksgiving

Happy St. Patrick's Day

Happy Halloween
Enjoy the turkey

Happy Easter

Happy Anniversary

Happy 4ᵗʰ of July

So sorry to hear you're sick

Happy Labor Day

Escape the hospital

Thank you

Cat hair makes quilts softer

SUPPLIERS - Most craft and variety stores carry an excellent assortment of supplies. If you need something special, ask your local store to contact the following companies:
POST CARD BACKING FABRIC
  Design Originals, 800-877-7820, www.d-originals.com
STEAM-A-SEAM 2
  Warm Co., 206-320-9276, Seattle, WA
PELLON
  Pellon, 678-526-7900, Lithonia, GA
CRAFT & APPLIQUE SHEET
  www.prairiegrovepeddler.com
EMBROIDERY FLOSS & PEARL COTTON
  DMC, 973-589-0606, S. Kearny, NJ
  Weeks Dye Works, 877-683-7393, Garner, NC

Let's get together and quilt

MANY THANKS to my friends for their cheerful help and wonderful ideas!
Kathy McMillan
Jennifer Laughlin
Lisa Vollrath
Janet Long
David & Donna Thomason